NEW VOYAGES IN ENGLISH

New Voyages in English

By Francis B. Connors

and a committee
of English teachers

LOYOLA UNIVERSITY PRESS
Chicago   60657

ACKNOWLEDGMENTS

"Hey, Bug!" from I FEEL THE SAME WAY by Lilian Moore. Text copyright © 1967 by Lilian Moore. Reprinted by permission of Atheneum Publishers. "What is Yellow?" from HAILSTONES AND HALIBUT BONES by Mary O'Neil. © 1961 by Mary Le Duc O'Neil. Reprinted by permission of Doubleday & Company, Inc. "Jump or Jiggle" from ANOTHER HERE AND NOW STORY BOOK edited by Lucy S. Mitchell. © 1937 by E. P. Dutton & Co., Inc. Copyright renewal © 1965 by Lucy Sprague Mitchell. Reprinted by permission of the publisher, E. P. Dutton. "Sudden Storm" from THE SPARROW BUSH by Elizabeth Coatsworth. © 1966 by Elizabeth Coatsworth. Used by permission of Grosset & Dunlap, Inc. "Jim" from BRONZEVILLE BOYS AND GIRLS by Gwendolyn Brooks. © 1956 by Gwendolyn Brooks Blakely. By permission of Harper & Row, Publishers, Inc. "Spring" and "Tiptoe" from IN THE MIDDLE OF THE TREES by Karla Kuskin. © 1958 by Karla Kuskin. By permission of Harper & Row, Publishers, Inc. "Rope Rhyme" from HONEY, I LOVE by Eloise Greenfield. © 1978 by Thomas Y. Crowell Company. By permission of the author. "Alligator Pie" from ALLIGATOR PIE by Dennis Lee. © 1974 by Dennis Lee. Reprinted by permission of Houghton Mifflin Company and the Macmillan Company of Canada. "What Shall I Pack in the Box Marked Summer?" by Bobbi Katz. © 1970 by Bobbi Katz. Reprinted by permission of the author. "How Creatures Move" reprinted with permission from the book A SMALL CHILD'S BOOK OF VERSE by P. Doane, © 1948. Published by David McKay Co., Inc. "The Strangers" from CHALLENGE TO TIME AND DEATH by Audrey A. Brown. © 1943 by Audrey A. Brown. Reprinted by permission of the Macmillan Company of Canada. "Emma's Store" by Dorothy Aldis. Reprinted by permission of G. P. Putnam's Sons from ALL TOGETHER by Dorothy Aldis. Copyright 1925, 1926, 1927, 1928, 1934, 1939, 1952; renewed 1953, 1954, 1955, 1956, 1962, and 1967 by Dorothy Aldis. "Meg's Egg" by Mary Ann Hoberman from *Cricket Magazine for Children*, Vol. 3, No. 3. © 1975 by Mary Ann Hoberman. Reprinted by permission of Russell & Volkening, Inc., as agent for the author. Definitions of "drummer" and "gold" from SCOTT, FORESMAN BEGINNING DICTIONARY by E. L. Thorndike and Clarence L. Barnhart. © 1979 by Scott, Foresman and Company. Reprinted by permission.

And grateful acknowledgment to:

Scott, Foresman and Company for "The Squirrel" from THE ARBUTHNOT ANTHOLOGY FOR CHILDREN, edited by May Hill Arbuthnot. © 1961. Charles Scribner's Sons for "The Duel" by Eugene Field from POEMS OF CHILDHOOD, copyright © 1932. Xerox Educational Publications for "The Little Girl Who Wouldn't Say Please" from *St. Nicholas Magazine*, 1895.

In some cases it has been extremely difficult to trace the authors and publishers of poems. If by chance we have been guilty of neglect in acknowledging our obligations, we trust our honest endeavors will be accepted as our apology.

Cover photo by Kenneth Garrett, Woodfin Camp, Inc., Washington, D.C.

Illustrated by Carol Tornatore

Preface

It is no doubt true that students grow toward maturity and independence of thought as they progress through the grades; but this growth is not as a rule a sharp and sudden one, nor does the psychology of the students undergo any great change during the various levels of learning in school. Methods, general objectives, and certainly the fundamental principles that underlie the work of the school remain the same from year to year. The need in every level is to bring about academic growth by providing new and broader experiences.

Students can grow in school only if they are active. They must therefore be interested in their own lives. The first and most obvious thing that they can do is to discuss their lives with others. Such communication should be encouraged and done naturally and joyfully. If they feel that the group finds value in what they have to say, they will wish more and more to express themselves well. The students are given models of written expression that will help to make them sensitive to beauty of word and phrase. They are taught to use certain methods and to observe certain rules; these are accepted because they find that the methods and the rules are things that easily can be understood and used in their oral and written work.

NEW VOYAGES IN ENGLISH, insofar as a textbook can accomplish such a purpose, endeavors to create a classroom atmosphere conducive to a group spirit. All should be made to feel that the entire group is interested in what each has to say. They should listen courteously and criticize in a polite and constructive manner.

It is also necessary to supply the students with new experiences. Schools can do this by means of motion pictures, excursions, and other similar activities. A textbook can do so only by encouraging the reading of books and by the models and exercises it contains. NEW VOYAGES IN ENGLISH conscientiously excludes from its model paragraphs and from the sentences in its exercises whatever is misanthropic, destructive, or psychologically harmful. The world that it seeks to create in the classroom is a bright world, a happy world, and a usefully busy world.

Students can tell of their experiences either orally or in written form. The authors accept as a fundamental principle that oral expression should precede written expression. Expression, whether oral or written, should provide variety, stimulate the imagination, and inspire creative effort by taking different forms. Students can express themselves by telling the class of something they have read, by taking part in discussions, by class dramatizations of things read in books, by imaginary broadcasts, telecasts, and telephone calls, by writing a paragraph or by writing a letter. It has been the aim of the authors to make use of every form of expression that has been found to be practical and appealing.

The authors believe very wholeheartedly in the student-centered school, but only if that term is properly understood. Students are necessarily the center of the school's activity, for everything that the school undertakes, every activity in which it engages, has for its immediate object the doing of something to or for the students; nor can the school afford to forget, in any of its planning, what the students need to achieve and what the students are capable of achieving. The school should be centered around the students in the sense that it accepts their growth as something to be sought in everything that it does. But this growth need not be undirected. Rather, it should be planned by those who have the training and experience to recognize the great potential of wisely directed students. This direction is something that students today need, something they desire, and something that they willingly accept if nothing has ever occurred to destroy their confidence.

The growth that is sought in NEW VOYAGES IN ENGLISH is one toward an adulthood that is truly cultured, that accepts social service as a duty, and that can render social service the better because students have been taught to think clearly and to express themselves effectively.

Lying before the students who are to arrive at this destination is a long voyage. The authors cannot hope to have taken the students a great distance. It will be enough for them if they can feel that they have given the students seaworthy ships and started them on their way. To have done this much—even to have made a sincere attempt at doing it—is no small thing in a day when, for many individuals, there is no sound vessel in which to sail, no known port of call, no compass, and no stars visible through the ragged clouds by which to chart a course.

Contents

CHAPTER THREE   **Writing About
Free Time Fun   45**

CHAPTER SIX   Visits to Bookland 115

Contents

CHAPTER THREE   Verbs   201

PART ONE

CREATIVE ACTIVITIES

CHAPTER ONE

A Happy Family

There was once a young prince who set out on a search for true happiness. He believed that he would find it in some faraway land. His journey took him to many exciting places.

In grand castles he met noble kings and queens who owned riches and had power, but he did not find true happiness. He saw glittering cities and awesome mountains, but he only felt lonely. After traveling all over the world, he met a wise man who told him why he had failed.

"Return to your home," he said, "and live in love and kindness. There you will find true happiness."

The young man returned to his home. He and his family loved one another and treated everyone kindly. The young prince found true happiness at last.

COURTESY

Love and kindness bring happiness to our families. Read the following conversation. Notice how each member tried to treat others courteously.

MODEL: A FAMILY CONVERSATION

STEVE: Mom, our birthday is in two weeks!

SUSAN: Yes, and it is on a Saturday. May we have a party?

MOM: A party sounds great! What do you think, Dad?

DAD: Indeed they should have a party! Let's plan it now.

ANNE: Since Mom will be at work on Friday, I could make a cake when I get home from school.

STEVE: Thanks, Anne! Could you make one of your chocolate ones?

ANNE: Sure, I'll make any kind you'd like.

SUSAN: That's great! Your chocolate cakes are the best anywhere.

STEVE: Will we have ice cream?

MOM: Of course! What's a birthday party without ice cream?

STEVE: When will the party be?

MOM: Let's make it from two to five o'clock on Saturday afternoon.

DAD: I will help you decorate the family room on Saturday morning.

SUSAN: How many friends may we invite, Mom?

MOM: It's your eighth birthday, so each may invite eight guests.

STEVE: A party wouldn't be any fun without our little brother. We want you to be there, Dave.

DAVE: I like parties. Will I get any presents?

ANNE: No, Dave, you must wait for your own birthday.

SUSAN: I'll call cousin Carol after dinner. I hope she will come to our party.

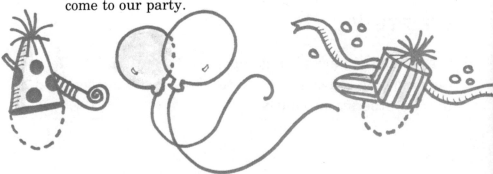

MOM: Make up your lists tonight, and call your friends when you come home from school tomorrow.

STEVE: Gary doesn't have a phone, and I want him to come to the party.

MOM: You'll have to send invitations to some of your guests, then.

SUSAN: I'll be happy to do that, Mom. I'm so glad it's almost my birthday.

These family members acted kindly and courteously with one another. They showed their love and were happy to please.

CLASS ASSIGNMENT

A Select three girls to read the parts of Mrs. Parker, Anne, and Susan, and three boys to be Mr. Parker, Steve, and Dave. Each should show by his voice the part he is reading.

B Write a conversation that might take place in your home when the members of your family talk about:

      1 Plans for a picnic

      2 Going to a movie

      3 A television program

Telephone Invitations

Susan and Steve hurried home from school the next day. They wanted to invite their friends to the party. Steve made the calls as Susan found the phone numbers. Listen as Steve invites Dianne Wagner to attend.

MODEL: TELEPHONE CALL –AN INVITATION

(Steve removes the receiver and dials the number.)

MRS. WAGNER: Mrs. Wagner speaking. Good afternoon.

STEVE: This is Steve Parker, Mrs. Wagner. I'd like to speak to Dianne.

MRS. WAGNER: Of course, Steve. Just a minute.

STEVE: Thank you. (Steve waits for Dianne to answer.)

DIANNE: This is Dianne, Hi!

STEVE: This is Steve Parker. Susan and I are having a birthday party Saturday, October 17, from two until five o'clock. Will you be one of our guests?

DIANNE: I'd like to go, Steve. I'll ask Mother. (Dianne asks her mother for permission to go to the party.) Hello, Steve. Yes, I may go. I'll be there at two o'clock on Saturday afternoon.

STEVE: I'm glad you can come. Dianne. Good-bye.

DIANNE: Thanks for the invitation! Bye!

CLASS ASSIGNMENT

A   Select three students to take the parts of Mrs. Wagner, Steve, and Dianne. Pretend there are two telephones in the room as they read the conversation.

B   Invite a friend to a cookout with your family on Friday. Study the rules for telephone invitations.

C   Invite your grandmother to dinner by telephone.

WHEN WE MAKE A TELEPHONE CALL:

1 We check the number in the telephone directory. (Your parents may do this for you.)
2 After removing the receiver, we dial the correct number.
3 The person answering tells who is speaking.
4 We give our name, then ask for the person we are calling.
5 We give our message clearly and briefly.
6 We are courteous. We speak in a friendly, cheerful voice.
7 When we have completed the call, we say, "Good-bye."

Greeting Guests

It was the twins' birthday, and the guests arrived at the Parker home at two o'clock. Steve and Susan welcomed their friends. Read what they said and learn how to speak politely with others.

MODEL: AT THE PARTY

(The doorbell rings; Steve opens the door.)

STEVE: Hello, Carol, I'm glad you could come.
CAROL: Happy birthday, Steve, and a happy birthday to you, Susan.
SUSAN: This is one of the happiest birthdays Steve and I have ever had! I hope you enjoy our party. Let me take your coat and hat.
MRS. PARKER: Hello, Carol. I'm glad you came early.
CAROL: Hello, Aunt Lucy. I came with mother. She is going

to stop in on the way home. Here is a present for you, Susan. And this one is for Steve.

SUSAN: Thank you! We will open our gifts at three o'clock. There's the doorbell again. (She goes to the door to greet the new arrival.) Hello, Rosa, welcome to our party!

ROSA: I'm glad that you invited me! Here is a game you can both enjoy.

STEVE: Thank you, Rosa. We like games. I'll take your coat.

SUSAN (Leading Rosa toward her mother): Mother, this is my new friend, Rosa Montez.

MRS. PARKER (Putting out her hand): How do you do, Rosa. I have heard the twins speak of you. I'm glad to meet you.

ROSA (Shaking hands with Susan's mother): I am glad to meet you, too.

MRS. PARKER: Enjoy yourself, dear. You know most of the children, I think. This is Susan's cousin, Carol Morse. Carol, meet Rosa Montez.

CAROL: Hi, Rosa. You're the new girl in Susan's class. I've heard her speak of you.

ROSA: I'm happy to meet you, Carol. I really feel that I know you, too.

Introductions

Mrs. Parker did not know one of the girls at the party. Susan introduced Rosa to her mother. Susan spoke her mother's name first. It is proper to say the name of an older person first. Say the girl's name first when introducing a boy to a girl. When two girls or two boys are introduced, either name may be mentioned first.

CLASS ASSIGNMENT

A Select students in your class to be Mrs. Parker, Susan, Rosa and Carol. Have them act out the introductions that were made at the twins' birthday party.

    1 How many introductions were made at the party?

    2 In introducing Rosa, whose name was mentioned first? Why?

B What would you say if you were introducing your friend, Joseph, to your father?

TALKING TOGETHER

Steve and Susan often talk with other boys and girls. Sometimes all the children in class talk about one subject. Their teacher guides the conversation so that they will stick to the topic. Listen to their conversation about a classroom fair.

MODEL: A CLASS CONVERSATION

TEACHER: Next month we are going to have an Around the World Fair. We hope to share information about the history and culture of people from other lands. What should we include in our Fair?

TERESA: A family from Japan just moved onto our street. I'm sure Mrs. Nakamoto will let me bring in her kimono, which is typical clothing for many Japanese women.

TEACHER: Fine, Teresa. I'm sure you will explain how important the kimono is in Japan.

SILVIA: My grandmother lives in Lisbon, the capital of Portugal. I can show slides from my trip there last summer. You will see oxcarts piled high with cork from the oak forests there.

TEACHER: Most of the cork used in the world comes from Portugal, Silvia. This kind of sharing helps us to understand how we help one another and how much we need one another.

MARK: Last year I read an African folk tale that I really enjoyed. Maybe we could tell folk tales and legends from different countries.

TONY: I can sing an Italian folk song, and Maria can play it on the accordion.

TEACHER: Every Fair should have some music, Tony. I think that's an excellent idea.

HELENA: I know the flag of Sweden has a large yellow cross which appears on a blue field. Some of us could research and even make flags to display.

ROBERTO: What is a Fair without food? My parents are from Mexico and my Mom makes spicy tamales. I'll ask her to make some for the class.

TEACHER: You have many excellent ideas for the Fair. Everyone can sign up for a particular project, then share your progress with the class. We can invite Mr. Green's class to come to the Fair.

CLASS ASSIGNMENT

Choose one of the following subjects for a class conversation. Ask your teacher to be the leader.

> Planning a class field trip
> What I do at a Halloween party
> What I want to be when I grow up

In a Class Conversation:

1 *There is a leader who guides the conversation.*
2 *Each student tries to say something about the subject.*
3 *Each student speaks in a loud, clear voice.*
4 *Students do not interrupt one another. They wait until the one who is speaking has finished.*

Dialogues

A dialogue is a conversation between two or more persons.

Did you ever hear two birds calling to each other from the treetops, or a mother hen scolding her little chicks? Sometimes we pretend that animals really can talk, and that we can understand them.

Edward Lear wrote a poem about an owl and a pussy cat, in which the animals talk to each other. Use a dancing voice when you say this poem, because it is a nonsense song. Words which may be new to you are *five-pound note, shilling, quince* and *runcible spoon*. The five-pound note and the shilling are kinds of English money. Quince is a small, hard yellow fruit like an apple that is used in marmalade and jellies. A runcible spoon is a small fork, such as we use with pickles.

THE OWL AND THE PUSSY-CAT
by Edward Lear

The Owl and the Pussy-Cat went to sea
   In a beautiful pea-green boat;
They took some honey, and plenty of money,
   Wrapped up in a five-pound note.
The Owl looked up to the stars above,
   And sang to a small guitar:

What a beautiful Pussy you are,
   You are,
   You are!
What a beautiful Pussy you are!"

Pussy said to the Owl, "You elegant fowl!
    How charmingly sweet you sing!
Oh let us be married! too long we have tarried:
    But what shall we do for a ring?"
They sailed away for a year and a day,
    To the land where the Bong-tree grows;
And there in a wood a Piggy-wig stood,
    With a ring at the end of his nose,
        His nose,
        His nose,
    With a ring at the end of his nose.

"Dear Pig, are you willing to sell for one shilling
    Your ring?" Said the Piggy, "I will."
So they took it away, and were married next day
    By the Turkey who lives on the hill.
They dined on mince, and slices of quince,
    Which they ate with a runcible spoon;
And hand in hand, on the edge of the sand,
    They danced by the light of the moon,
        The moon,
        The moon,
    They danced by the light of the moon.

14

After reading "The Owl and the Pussy-Cat," the class decided they would do animal dialogues. Steve Parker remembered the story of the lion that was kind to a mouse and had his life saved in return. Their teacher asked Steve to take the part of the lion and asked Susan to pretend she was the mouse. This was their conversation:

MODEL: A DIALOGUE

LION: How fortunate that you came along this path at the right time! I am caught in this rope trap and fear I will surely be in some zoo next month.

MOUSE: Don't worry! I shall gnaw through those ropes.

LION: Ah! Now I am free to roam the jungles again! Many thanks, little fellow. I am grateful to you for releasing me.

MOUSE: You once saved my life in this great jungle. One good turn deserves another. Enjoy your freedom!

CLASS ASSIGNMENT

A Give the following dialogues in your classroom:

1 A dog and a spider speak.

DOG: Sigh. Everyone has gone out and I'm home alone.

SPIDER: You're not alone!

DOG: Where did that little voice come from? Who are you?

SPIDER: I'm a small spider over here in the corner. I've seen you before and wanted to be your friend. Would you like to watch me make a beautiful web?

DOG: Thank you, I would like that very much. I'm glad to have a new friend and to know I'm not alone.

2 A worm and a garter snake talk.

WORM: Ever since the first day I saw you I have been trying to be like you. I eat and eat and I stretch and stretch. But how can I become green?

SNAKE: Oh, silly worm, you will never be green!

WORM: But if I can't be green, I can never be just like you.

SNAKE: That's true. You will always be yourself, but there is nothing wrong with that. When I was little, I sometimes wished I could stay small as a worm does and hide in the cool earth. Now I have learned to be content as I am, and that is what you should do, too.

WORM: You're right. I should discover the things that are special about myself and be the best worm I can be.

3 An alley cat and a raccoon speak.

CAT: If you are a cat, you are the biggest one I have ever seen!

RACCOON: Hello, fellow scavenger. No, I'm not a cat. I'm a raccoon. Most of us live in the country, but my family and some others have ventured into the city.

CAT: It's a hard life here in the alleys.

RACCOON: Yes, but we heard there was a possibility of great riches. Stories have been told of finding roast beef, flounder, and marshmallows.

CAT: I've seen little of such things. But I will be glad to show you the alleys behind the best restaurants. You may try your luck with the rest of us.

4   Two cows converse.

1ST COW: How now, brown cow?

2ND COW: You always say that when you see me! Let's go over by the fence. We can talk about those trespassers in our meadow.

1ST COW: Do you mean the ducks down by the river?

2ND COW: Yes, the ones that arrived last night. I am sure they are on their way south for the winter. I wonder what they are like.

1ST COW: Instead of talking about them, we should go down and welcome them. They must be tired after their journey.

2ND COW: Of course we should greet them! I wasn't being thoughtful. Perhaps there is something we can do to help them.

B   Tiger, a cat, invited his friends to a birthday party. Each animal has a special way of walking and talking. Can you supply the missing words in these sentences?

Which animal walks this way?

1   The_____gallops.   4   The_____flies.
2   The_____waddles.   5   The_____swims.
3   The_____hops.   6   The_____crawls.

How do these animals "talk"?

1 The dog _____ .   4 The duck _____ .
2 The pig _____ .   5 The lion _____ .
3 The cat _____ .   6 The cow _____ .

Write a dialogue showing the exact words spoken by Tiger and any of his guests as he welcomed them to the party.

C Think of what any of the following animals might say to each other. Choose a classmate to work with you, and prepare a dialogue between.

1 Two puppies playing in the backyard for the first time
2 An elephant and a mouse
3 A horse and a zebra
4 Two monkeys in a zoo
5 Two squirrels gathering nuts for the winter

PANTOMIMES

Everyone enjoys games and sports. Boys and girls like football, baseball, hockey, hopscotch, or jumping rope. They also play games of make-believe. Sometimes they pretend they are cowboys, airplane pilots, explorers, nurses, or teachers.

A kind of make-believe game children like is called pantomime. In it, we tell a story by the motions of our arms, hands, fingers, legs, and body. We express joy, surprise, or sadness in facial expressions. A pantomime is like a silent motion picture.

Steve and Susan's class enjoyed pantomimes. One student might give a pantomime by himself, or several children might work together on one. Here is a pantomime Jeremy Davis gave:

MODEL: A PANTOMIME

Jeremy held both his hands tightly over his right shoulder as if he were holding a stick. He watched a make-believe object sailing through the air toward him. Then he moved his hands forward, swinging with all his might. He dropped what he was holding and ran to the right. The expression on his face seemed to say, "I hit it."

Jeremy's pantomime was well done. His classmates knew at once that he had made a base hit.

MODEL: ANOTHER PANTOMIME

Marsha sat on a chair making a cradle with her arms. She rocked an imaginary object. Moving her lips, she pretended to sing.

CLASS ASSIGNMENT

A What was Marsha doing in this pantomime? Present the two models in your classroom. See if you can add actions of your own.

B   Select one of the following pantomimes and give it before your classmates:

1   Pretend you are the traffic officer at a busy corner.
2   Pretend you are jumping rope.
3   Pretend you are playing hopscotch.
4   Pretend you are ice skating.
5   Pretend you are playing basketball.
6   Pretend you are playing music. One student plays a violin, another a drum, and so forth. One director beats time.
7   Pretend you are playing a game, such as "Farmer in the Dell," "London Bridge," or "Pin the Tail on the Donkey."

GIVING A TALK

After doing the pantomimes, the children wanted to talk about their favorite pastimes. Their teacher told each child to prepare a talk about a game or a sport.

The twins watched their Dad plan an automobile trip by using a road map. He was able to choose the route which would take him straight to where he was going. Steve and Susan decided they needed a map to keep them going straight from the beginning of their talk to the end. This guide would tell them what to say in the opening sentence, how to continue the story, and how to end their talk. They called it an outline.

This was Steve's outline:

Beginning Sentence: My favorite pastime.
Middle Sentences: What I do.
Ending Sentence: How happy I am in doing it.

Using this outline, Steve prepared a talk about his favorite pastime, flying a kite.

FLYING HIGH

Flying a homemade kite is my favorite pastime. When the wind is strong, I send it for a long ride. As I move about the vacant lot, the wind blows the kite higher and higher. When I feel it pulling at the end of the string, I feel successful.

The class decided that Steve had given a most interesting talk. He explained about his outline and how it had helped him. In the future all his classmates made outlines for their talks.

CLASS ASSIGNMENT

A   Tell the class about a game you like. Plan your talk by making an outline before you begin.

B   Prepare a talk about one of the following:
1   An exciting event   4   Something I made
2   My favorite sport   5   A visit to the zoo
3   A TV show I like   6   A trip I took

Points to Remember

When you are speaking, the listener knows you have made a statement when you lower your voice and stop. In asking a question, your voice should go up. If you call some-one by name, pause a little before continuing. Occasionally show excitement or joy in your voice. Read these sentences aloud, and listen to your own voice.

> Will you go to the park with me?
> I like your new hat.
> Eric, please help me carry this big box.
> That building is on fire!

Remember the punctuation marks used in writing sentences—a period when you lower your voice and stop; a question mark when raising the voice; a comma for a slight pause; and an exclamation point for a strong feeling.

Every sentence begins with a capital letter.

The following jingle may help you remember this:

> I'm a capital letter;
> I'm at your service, you see.
> Whenever you write a sentence,
> Begin the first word with me.

CHORAL SPEAKING

There is music in poetry. We hear the music best when a poem is spoken. We shall recite poems together, trying to sound like one voice. Reciting poems together is called "choral speaking."

Let us practice making our voices sound like one voice by reading "Sudden Storm." Imagine walking down a street in your town when suddenly it begins to rain. Colorful umbrellas pop up everywhere, as people try to stay dry. This poem describes a scene just like that. Let us say it together, pronouncing each word distinctly.

SUDDEN STORM
by Elizabeth Coatsworth

The rain comes in sheets,
Sweeping the streets;
Here, here, and here,
Umbrellas appear.
Red, blue, yellow, green,
They tilt and they lean
Like mushrooms, like flowers
That grow when it showers.

Now that we have learned to speak well together, let us say another poem. "What Shall I Pack in the Box Marked 'Summer'?" tells us one poet's happy memories of summertime. Do you remember some of the same things? What else do you like best about summer?

WHAT SHALL I PACK IN THE BOX MARKED "SUMMER"?
by Bobbi Katz

A handful of wind that I caught with a kite,
A firefly's flame in the dark of the night,
The green grass of June that I tasted with toes,
The flowers I knew from the tip of my nose,
The clink of the ice cubes in pink lemonade,
The fourth of July Independence parade!
The sizzle of hot dogs, and fizzle of coke,
Some pickles and mustard and barbecue smoke,
The print of my fist in the palm of my mitt,
As I watched for the batter to strike out or hit,
The splash of the water, the top-to-toe cool
Of a stretch-and-kick trip through a blue swimming pool,
The tangle of night songs that slipped through my screen
Of crickets and insects too small to be seen,
The seed pods that formed on the flowers to say
That summer was packing her treasures away.

Mrs. English

CHAPTER TWO

New Lessons
in School

Susan and Steve liked school. They made many new friends there. One friend was their teacher. On the first day of school she wrote her name on the chalkboard.

Mrs. English

She taught the children how to pronounce her name and how to spell it. Mrs. English told the boys and girls to write her name on a slip of paper for their parents.

> **The first letter of a person's name begins with a capital letter.**

The teacher told the children to write their names on slips of paper. She explained that she would call each child by his or her correct name and that they should call her Mrs. English.

LEARNING THE PARAGRAPH

Steve and Susan liked to talk with their classmates. The conversation in the schoolyard was all about the birthday party, especially what each guest did with the paper hat received at the party. Nancy Brooks said she pasted it in her scrapbook.

Whenever Nancy put something in her scrapbook, she wrote an explanation beside it. She wrote this beside the hat she received at the twins' birthday party.

Today I had a wonderful time at the birthday party of Susan and Steve Parker. We played games and sang songs. This is the favor I received. It will remind me of the fun I had.

The sentences which Nancy wrote form a *paragraph*.

A paragraph is a group of sentences telling about *one thing*. The sentences in Nancy's paragraph tell about the birthday party she attended. You will want to learn about writing paragraphs, too. The first thing to remember is that all the sentences in a paragraph tell about one thing.

The sentences of a paragraph are written one after another, just as Nancy wrote in her scrapbook.

In the paragraph on the next page, notice that all the sentences tell about the fun Petunia has playing with a windup mouse. How many sentences are there in this paragraph?

FUN FOR PETUNIA

My kitten, Petunia, enjoys playing with her new windup mouse. She runs after it when I send it across the room. When it stops, she gives it a little push with her paw. For Petunia, chasing something is much more fun than catching it.

CLASS ASSIGNMENT

What is the *one thing* talked about in these paragraphs? Copy one paragraph in your notebook.

1   *OUR HELPERS*

The children in our school have special helpers. They stand at street corners at dismissal making sure that students cross over safely. How lucky we are to have these crossing guards to help us.

2   *NEEDLESS FEAR*

My baby sister is afraid of our new puppy. Whenever she hears his gruff bark, she hides behind Grandfather's chair. If Amy only knew how gentle Tramp is, she would not be scared.

Parts of a Paragraph

A paragraph has three parts: (1) a beginning sentence, (2) middle sentences, and (3) an ending sentence. The *beginning sentence* is the first sentence, or topic sentence. It gives a hint of what we are going to talk about. The *middle sentences* tell more about the topic. These sentences help a

28

paragraph grow. The *ending sentence* is the last sentence. Sometimes it tells the last thing that happened, but it may also ask a question or express a thought about the topic of the paragraph.

Study the three paragraph parts in the following model:

MODEL: A STRANGE SPINNER

Beginning Sentence: Silk is spun by a caterpillar-like
Middle Sentences: silkworm. This insect lives where
                            the climate is warm and moist. It
Ending Sentence: eats mulberry leaves. Isn't it strange
                            that such a tiny creature can spin a
                            thread of beautiful silk?

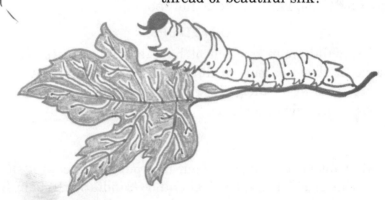

CLASS ASSIGNMENT

A Answer these questions about the paragraph "A Strange Spinner":
   1 How many sentences are there?
   2 What is the topic mentioned in the beginning sentence?
   3 Do the middle sentences tell more about the silkworm?
   4 What is the ending sentence?

B Point out the beginning, the middle, and the ending sentences in each of the following paragraphs. What is the *one thing* talked about in each?

1   *A BROWN GHOST*

The old tree growing in our yard has changed its looks again. The leaves have fallen to the ground. All the branches are brown and bare. Now it looks like an ugly old ghost.

2   *WINDOWS*

The windows in our classroom are like shining eyes. They watch the busy streets below. On clear days they can see the whole town. When I am coming to school, I feel as if they are friendly eyes welcoming me.

3   *MY FAVORITE FRUIT*

An apple is my favorite fruit. I eat one for lunch every day. I wish we had an apple tree in our yard.

4   *GOOD FRIENDS*

Our teeth work very hard for us. They grind our food, making it easy to swallow. Without these helpers, we could not digest our meals properly.

C The following sentences make a paragraph, because they tell about one thing. Copy the sentences and write them in correct paragraph form.

Steve and Susan received many gifts for their birthday. They had fun trying to guess what was in each package. The twins remembered to thank their friends for their lovely presents.

D The following sentences tell about one thing. They are not in proper order. Copy the sentences in the correct order to form a paragraph.

The first American was in space at last! The astronaut waited for the countdown. A mighty roar was heard. Soon the rocket zoomed into the sky.

WRITING ABOUT PETS

Steve and Susan were very fond of their pet dog, Pickle. They often told their classmates about his tricks. Other children in the class had pets—cats, hamsters, fish, dogs, rabbits, gerbils, white mice, and birds. The children wanted to write paragraphs describing their pets.

Making an Outline

When we describe a pet, we tell what it looks like. The children decided to tell in the beginning sentence what kind of pet they had. In the middle sentences they gave details about its appearance. They ended the paragraph by telling how much they liked their pet. This is the *outline* they used for writing their paragraphs:

Beginning Sentence: What kind of pet I have
Middle Sentences: What my pet looks like
Ending Sentence: How much I like my pet

Building a Vocabulary

Many children in the class had dogs for pets. These are some words they used in writing their paragraphs:

KIND OF DOG	COLOR	OTHER WORDS FOR DOG	HAIR
setter	black		shaggy
terrier	tan and white	companion	soft
bulldog	spotted	friend	wiry
spaniel	white	playmate	silky
collie	dark brown	protector	smooth
shepherd	reddish brown	watchdog	fluffy

EARS

tiny
pointed
floppy
droopy
broad

KIND OF EYES

sad
bright
intelligent
friendly
kind

TAIL

long
stubby
bushy
curly
short

WHAT I THINK HE OR SHE IS

faithful
naughty
playful
clever

The Beginning Sentence

The *beginning sentence* is the first sentence in a paragraph. It gives a hint of what we are going to talk about. We should make the beginning sentence interesting and attractive, so that people will want to read the whole paragraph.

In the beginning sentence the children told what kind of pet they had. These topic sentences were suggested:

1 McCloud is a lovable black scotch terrier.
2 Jip is a handsome white collie.
3 Tatters is just a friendly stray dog I found on the street.
4 Tramp is a frisky little poodle.

CLASS ASSIGNMENT

A Here are ten beginning sentences. Read each sentence. Tell what you think the topic of the paragraph would be.
1 I always enjoy the Fourth of July parade.
2 A robin built a nest in our apple tree.
3 Windy days were made for flying kites.
4 One day my dog got into trouble with our neighbor's cat.
5 Last night, as I was studying my lessons, I heard a strange noise in the closet.
6 Squirrels are busy animals in autumn.
7 Raking leaves is an autumn chore.
8 On my birthday Mother surprised me.
9 My first attempt at ice-skating was funny to watch.
10 Yesterday my brother took his first trumpet lesson.

B Write a beginning sentence for each of these paragraphs. The suggestions after the first paragraph will help you write a good sentence.

1   *THE PRETZEL MAN*

_____ . He stands at the corner near Wilson School with his warm pretzels for sale. Even when we don't buy anything, his happy smile cheers our day.

WHEN?	WHAT?	WHOM?
Every afternoon	speak	friendly face
On our way home from school	call	familiar figure
As we come home from school	greet	peddler
When we leave our school	see	street vendor

2   *LIVE SNOWMEN*

_____ . Because it is so cold where they live, they dress in suits of skin and fur to keep warm. Their homes are round houses built of blocks of ice. If I were an Eskimo, I would tire of ice and snow.

C   Does the beginning sentence of this paragraph make you want to read more? Does it tell what the topic of the paragraph is?

ENCHANTED NIGHT

Beginning Sentence: Halloween night is a ghostly one. The moon plays hide-and-seek with the black clouds. Goblins, witches, and ghosts fly through the air. Are you frightened on Halloween night?

Middle Sentences

We have learned that the beginning sentence of a paragraph gives a hint of what is to follow. The *middle sentences* tell more about the topic. In the model paragraph, the beginning sentence tells us that the topic is the *appearance* of the pet. So the middle sentences should tell more about what the pet *looks* like.

Our paragraphs may have two or more middle sentences. Each of these sentences tells something about the topic. How many middle sentences are there in the model "My Pal" below?

Philip Connors used the vocabulary and suggested beginning sentences to write this paragraph. He named it "My Pal." Did he follow the outline? Do you know what his dog looks like from reading his paragraph?

MODEL: MY PAL

Jip, my faithful pal, is a handsome white collie. He has bright, intelligent eyes and a long, pointed nose. His thick, bushy tail is curly on the end. I am glad to have a friend like Jip.

Do the two middle sentences tell something more about the pet's appearance?

CLASS ASSIGNMENT

A Does the following paragraph describe a pet? Does it tell about one animal? How many middle sentences are there?

BALL OF GOLD

My hamster looks like a soft golden ball. Short golden-brown fur covers his little round body. He has alert brown eyes in his gentle face. I am happy to have Butterscotch for a pet.

B Read this paragraph and then answer the questions below:

PINKIE

Would you like to know why I called my new rabbit Pinkie? Beneath his soft white fur his little body is pink. His broad ears are lined with pink. A pink dot forms his nose. Even his bright eyes seem pink. Don't you think I named him well?

1 How many reasons did the writer give for naming her rabbit Pinkie?
2 Is this paragraph about *one thing*? What is the one thing?
3 How many middle sentences are there in this paragraph?
4 With what kind of sentence does this paragraph end?
5 Why is the beginning sentence a good sentence?

Misfit Sentences

A paragraph tells about one thing. When we write about the appearance of a pet, every sentence in the paragraph must tell something about the appearance of the pet. A sentence which does not develop the topic of the paragraph is a *misfit sentence*. It does not fit in the paragraph.

There is a misfit sentence in the following paragraph. It is printed in italics. When we read this paragraph carefully, we can see that the misfit sentence does not tell anything about the appearance of the pet.

A HANDSOME PET

I have a handsome chestnut pony for a pet. His brown coat is smooth and glossy. His eyes are large and dark. *Sometimes I give him a lump of sugar after he eats his oats and hay.* Strong, slender legs support his sturdy body. I am very lucky to be able to have my own horse.

The Ending Sentence

The last sentence in a paragraph is called the *ending sentence*. This sentence must finish the paragraph. It may tell the last thing that happened or may add a personal comment.

A sentence expressing what we think or feel about the topic often makes a good ending sentence. These ending sentences were suggested by the twins' classmates:

1 Wouldn't you like to have a friend like mine?
2 I think he is the best watchdog in the world.
3 Tatters is not very handsome, but he is my favorite playmate.
4 Now you know why I love my puppy.

We should remember that a good ending sentence really finishes the paragraphs and should please the people who read it. Read the paragraph on the next page and answer these questions:

1 Name the three parts of this paragraph.
2 How many middle sentences are in this paragraph?
3 Do you like the ending sentence? Does it really finish the paragraph?

MY FURRY FRIEND

Tatters is just a friendly stray dog I found on the street. His sad, kind eyes and his droopy ears made me like him at once. His curly tail wags his happiness. Tatters is not very handsome, but he is my favorite playmate.

CLASS ASSIGNMENT

Read this paragraph silently, then have a class discussion about it. Is the ending sentence a good one? It is an exclamatory sentence.

LOST

The last time my uncle took me to the woods, something unpleasant happened. While he was cutting down a fir tree, I pretended to be a bear. I hid behind the trees and made a cave in the snow. When I stopped, I couldn't see my uncle anywhere. I was frightened when he didn't answer my call. **Ending Sentence:** I ran to the top of the hill, and was relieved to see my uncle coming toward me!

Naming the Paragraph

A paragraph is not finished until we give it a name. We call this the *title*. If our title is attractive, people will want to read our paragraph. These are titles suggested by the class for stories about their pets:

Mischief Maker	A Perfect Puppy
My Pal	Flying Feathers
Fish Story	Fuzzy Companion
My Shadow	Fine Furry Friend

CLASS ASSIGNMENT

Read the following paragraphs silently. Do you like the titles?

GHOST-LIKE FACE

Last night Muff was in trouble again. Her ghost-like face and dusty fur told the story. White tracks on the floor led Mother to the kitchen. She soon discovered that Muff had knocked over an open box of cornstarch. Some of it had landed on Muff's head! My pet had a starchy bath.

SHY VISITOR

A bushy-tailed visitor hopped upon our windowsill to-day. He was looking for nuts to carry away to his secret hiding place. It was the same little squirrel that scampered up the nearest tree yesterday as I walked by. When food is available, however, that one is never shy!

ANOTHER WAY OF DESCRIBING A PET

Most of the children wrote paragraphs to describe their pets, but Rosa wrote a short rhyme about her kitten. This is how it looked.

SMUDGE

I have a cat the color of coal,
With four white paws and dainty toes,
Her fur is soft as soft can be.
I even love her turned-up nose.

This is called a rhyming poem because the words *toes* and *nose* rhyme; that is, they have the same sound. The children liked Rosa's rhyme and decided that they, too, could write rhymes about their pets.

Mrs. English told the children she thought it was best to start with only two lines. "Tom has a yellow canary for a pet," said Mrs. English. "Let us help him to write a rhyme about his pet. You may write the first line, Tom, then we will help you with the second line."

Tom wrote:

My pet is a yellow canary.

Mrs. English asked the students to think of words that rhymed with *canary*. Tom wrote on the chalkboard the words suggested by his classmates:

| merry | airy | very |
| hairy | Jerry | berry |

Mrs. English asked the students to give her a line that rhymed with *canary*. These were some of the suggested lines:

> I call him Jerry.
>
> He is jolly and merry.
>
> I fed him a berry.
>
> He's feathery, but not too hairy.

"Let us read the first line Tom wrote, then see which of these sentences fits best," said Mrs. English. "Would we have a good rhyme if we used the first suggestion? Say it aloud."

The class repeated the first rhyme:

> My pet is a yellow canary.
> I call him Jerry.

They decided it did not make a good rhyme because the first line had more syllables than the second. After trying each line suggested, they decided this was the best rhyme:

> My pet is a yellow canary,
> He's feathery, but not too hairy.

Here is another rhyme the children wrote:

> Acorn is my little gerbil pet,
> The cutest creature I ever met.

CLASS ASSIGNMENT

A   Select from the second, third, and fourth columns the words that rhyme with each word in the first column:

COLUMN 1	COLUMN 2	COLUMN 3	COLUMN 4
cold	fight	trip	glass
light	skip	brass	old
class	bold	hold	night
slip	pass	right	whip

B Name as many words as you can that rhyme with each of the following:

gate	park	round	jolly
away	glow	cat	bell

C Copy each rhyme. In the blank space at the end, write a word that rhymes with the last word in the first line.

   1 When Sadie, my kitten, chases her ball
     There's always one thing that you'll hear _____ .

   2 My cat is all gray and sleek.
     He likes to play hide-and- _____ .

   3 A short stubby tail has Duffy, my pup.
     He can't keep it down, it always flies _____ .

   4 My white and frisky little mouse
     Scampers all around her new _____ .

   5 A busy fellow is the bee,
     Making honey for you and _____ .

D Write second lines to rhyme with each of these first lines:

   1 My dog is all shaggy and white.

     _____ .

   2 I wish I had a little pig.

     _____ .

   3 I have a mouse as white as snow.

     _____ .

   4 My goldfish is a pretty thing.

     _____ .

   5 My duck is swimming in the pond.

     _____ .

CHORAL SPEAKING

Often we tell our parents how much we love them, but do we always show it in our actions? In the poem "Which Loved Best?" we hear the story of three children chatting with their mother.

WHICH LOVED BEST?
by Joy Allison

"I love you, Mother," said little John,
Then forgetting his work, his cap went on,
And he was off to the garden swing,
Leaving his mother the wood to bring.

"I love you, Mother," said little Nell,
"I love you better than tongue can tell."
Then she teased and pouted half the day,
Till Mother rejoiced when she went to play.

"I love you, Mother," said little Fan.
"Today, I'll help you all I can."
To the cradle then she did softly creep,
And rocked the baby till it fell asleep.

Then stepping softly, she took the broom,
And swept the floor and dusted the room;
Busy and happy all day was she,
Helpful and cheerful as child could be.

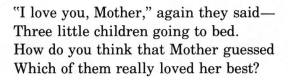

"I love you, Mother," again they said—
Three little children going to bed.
How do you think that Mother guessed
Which of them really loved her best?

Let the class say the poem together. One of the boys takes the part of John, saying the first four words. Then the entire class recites the rest of the stanza. Girls read the parts of Nell and Fan. In the last stanza, all three children say the first four words.

Try to make your voices sound like one voice. The students who take the parts of John, Nell, and Fan may add gestures when they say their lines.

All the children said they loved their mother, but John forgot to bring in the wood and Nell teased and pouted. Which child in the poem should we try to imitate? Why?

CHAPTER THREE

Writing About Free Time Fun

There are many ways of letting our classmates know about the fun we have in our free time. In this chapter we are going to write paragraphs about the wind, building a snowman, playing hide-and-seek, and how Christopher Columbus spent his free time as a little boy.

WRITING ABOUT THE WIND

One day Maria told Mrs. English that she could tell a true story about the wind. This is the story she told:

A TROUBLEMAKER

The wind played a mean trick on me today. I was helping my brother deliver newspapers, when a gust of wind suddenly snatched a paper out of my hands. It sailed high into the air like a magic carpet. The wind whirled it inside out, scattering the pieces all along the street. It took me a long time to pick up the torn sheets.

Mrs. English liked Maria's story. She asked her to write it on the chalkboard for the class to read. Then she asked the children what Maria's story was. Several students said it was a paragraph.

Other children had stories to tell about the tricks the wind had played on them. Mrs. English suggested that everyone write a paragraph about the wind.

Building a Vocabulary

The children talked about things the wind does. The teacher wrote these on the board.

WHAT THE WIND DOES

pushes people about
turns umbrellas inside out
helps boats to sail
snatches hats
blows branches off trees
rattles the windows

Mrs. English thought the children might want to tell what kind of wind was blowing and describe the sounds made by the wind. She asked them to think of words which would explain the kind of wind that was blowing and the sound it made. They would also need words to tell what they thought or felt about the topic. These are words suggested by the students:

KIND OF WIND	SOUNDS MADE BY THE WIND	OTHER WORDS FOR THE WIND
sharp	whistling	breeze
cold	puffing	windstorm
pleasant	singing	gust
blustering	howling	hurricane
rough	sighing	draft
playful	whispering	squall

Making an Outline

Before the students wrote their paragraphs, they made an outline. We remember that when Steve Parker gave a talk about his kite, he made an outline which helped him keep to the topic. Mrs. English's class made an outline to keep them going from the beginning of their paragraphs to the end. They decided the beginning sentence would mention something the wind did. The middle sentences would state more about what the wind did. The ending sentence would tell what the writer thought about the wind. This is the outline which each student followed as he wrote his paragraph:

Beginning Sentence: Something the wind did
Middle Sentences: What happened
Ending Sentence: What I think about the wind

Beginning Sentences

The class then talked about beginning sentences. They recalled that the *beginning sentence* should give a hint of the topic of the paragraph and should be interesting enough to attract attention. These sentences were suggested:

1 An invisible friend played with me.
2 The wind announced itself in a strong way today.
3 Last night I heard a rattling sound in our house.
4 Today the mischievous wind bothered everybody.
5 This morning the wind taught me a lesson.
6 On a rainy spring day, the blustering wind performed its favorite trick.

Middle Sentences

The *middle sentences* tell more about what is stated in the beginning sentence. Each sentence tells something about what the wind did.

The vocabulary that Mrs. English wrote on the chalkboard would be helpful in writing good middle sentences.

Ending Sentences

The *ending sentence* tells what the writer thought or felt about the wind. Mrs. English asked the children to suggest ending sentences which might be used. Here are their suggestions:

1 I had a good time with that playful wind.
2 The storm made me aware of the power of the wind.
3 That old wind will never scare me again.
4 The wind seemed to enjoy playing that game.
5 Would you like to be in a windstorm like that?
6 The wind must like rainy days.

Writing the Paragraph

Mrs. English's students were now ready to write a paragraph about the wind. They had a list of words to help them, and some beginning sentences on the board which they could use. Some children made up their own beginning sentences. In the middle sentences, they told more about the wind's behavior. They ended the paragraph by telling what they thought of the wind.

Here is a paragraph written by one child:

MY INVISIBLE FRIEND

Beginning Sentence:

Middle Sentences:

Ending Sentence:

> An invisible friend played with me last week. I was roller-skating outside on a windy afternoon. When I went up the block, the wind pushed against me and I had to skate very hard. But when I came back down the block, the wind pushed me from behind and I rolled along with no effort at all. I really had a good time with that playful wind.

Naming the Paragraph

The name of this paragraph is "My Invisible Friend." Mrs. English now asked the children to suggest other titles for stories about the wind. Here are some of them:

Ghosts?   Night Sounds
Gentle Breezes   Fun With the Wind
The Wind at Play   Sudden Squall

CLASS ASSIGNMENT

A   Write a paragraph telling about something you have seen the wind do.

B   Choose one of these situations, and write a paragraph telling what the wind did:
  1   A girl—an umbrella—a roof
  2   A boy—a kite—a tree
  3   A pile of papers—a desk—an open window
  4   A yard—a white sheet on the clothesline—a man walking by

C   Write an ending sentence for this paragraph:

THE WIND'S SECRET

   Last night I heard the wind whispering to the trees. What he told them must have been very funny. As they laughed, they shook so hard that many of their leaves tumbled to the ground._____ .

Misfit Sentences

   A paragraph tells about one thing. If we are writing about something the wind did, every sentence must tell about the wind's behavior. A sentence which does not tell about the topic of the paragraph is called a misfit sentence. It does not fit in the paragraph.

   There is a misfit sentence in the following paragraph. It is printed in italics. If we read this paragraph carefully, we see that the misfit sentence does not tell anything about the trick of the wind.

THE WIND AT PLAY

The wind played a bad trick on me as I was going to school this morning. *The wind whistles in the treetops.* It snatched my pretty new scarf and ran away with it. When I chased it, the wind tossed it into a mud puddle. Would you like to have the wind treat you in this way?

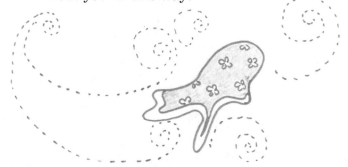

After we write a paragraph, we must read it carefully to see if there are any sentences which do not belong. If there are any misfit sentences, we must take them out.

CLASS ASSIGNMENT

A   Copy the paragraph "The Wind at Play," but leave out the misfit sentence.

B   Copy these paragraphs. Take out the misfit sentence in each paragraph.

THE WIND ON THE DUNES

We had a very unpleasant experience when we visited the dunes one day last summer. Just as we were finishing our lunch, the wind stirred up great clouds of sand. The food was delicious. My father ordered everyone to run to the car and close all the windows. Strong gusts beat against the car and drove sand through all the cracks. I hope I never get caught in a sandstorm again!

THAT MISCHIEVOUS WIND

What a good time the wind has on a rainy day! It blows the rain first one way and then another. It dashes into umbrellas and turns them inside out. Children are late for school. You can almost hear the wind laugh at the fun it is having.

C   Write middle sentences for the following paragraph. When you have finished, give it a title.

———————————————

I thought I saw ghostly shapes dancing in our back yard one night. ————————————————————————.

————————————————————————.

How glad I was to learn that the wind was only blowing some leaves on the tree in front of our street light.

WRITING ABOUT BUILDING A SNOWMAN

One day there was a heavy snowfall. As soon as school was out, some of the children ran to a vacant lot to build a snowman. First, they rolled the snow into two big round balls.

They placed one of these on top of the other for the body of the snowman. Then they made a smaller ball for his head. Stones formed his eyes, nose, and mouth. They found a rag which they used for a scarf, and an old hat for his head. One

of the children brought a pipe to stick in his mouth. The builders were very proud of their snowman.

When they told Mrs. English about the fun they had building the snowman, she said they could write a paragraph telling about it. With her help, they listed on the chalkboard the words they might use to tell how the snow looked, who built the snowman, what they did, the things they used, and how they felt.

Building a Vocabulary

Such lists of words are called a vocabulary. Students suggest words that are written on the chalkboard. Then all may select words from the lists to help them write well. Not every word is used in one paragraph.

HOW THE SNOW LOOKED

glistening
sparkling
soft
flaky
deep

WHO BUILT THE SNOWMAN

children
youngsters
playmates
friends
pals

WHAT THEY DID	THINGS USED	HOW THEY FELT
shoveled	shovels	happy
rolled	stones	laughing
stuck	snow	noisy
fastened	old hat	excited
piled	scarf	merry

Making an Outline

We have talked about many things that could be said about building a snowman. Now we will want to make an outline for our paragraph. This explains the order we are to follow in the beginning sentence, the middle sentences, and the ending sentence.

BUILDING A SNOWMAN

Beginning Sentence: Who built the snowman?
Middle Sentences: How was the snowman built?
Ending Sentence: How I feel about the results.

The Beginning Sentence

The beginning sentence is very important. In this sentence we should give a hint of what we are going to talk about in the paragraph. It should be so interesting that people will want to read the paragraph.

Mrs. English asked her students to suggest beginning sentences which might be used in a paragraph about building a snowman. The best sentences were written on the chalkboard:

1. Yesterday my pals and I had a great time building a snowman.
2. My cousins and I made a whole snow family yesterday.
3. After school yesterday my friends and I had fun building a snowman.
4. What a good time we had building a snowman.

The Middle Sentences

A paragraph may have several middle sentences that help develop the topic introduced by the beginning sentence. These sentences should be interesting, and should give one fact or detail after another in their natural order.

Always check your beginning sentence and your outline before writing your middle sentences. The middle sentences in this paragraph should tell how the snowman was built. Read the paragraph on **page 57.**

The Ending Sentence

The ending sentence may tell the last thing that happened, or it may express our feelings. It should please the readers and let them know that the story is ended.

These ending sentences were suggested by Mrs. English's students:

1. Is it any wonder that we welcome a snowstorm?
2. When we had finished, we were very proud of our sculpture.
3. After perching an old hat on his head, we were looking at a very funny figure.
4. Our snowman could almost pass for a real person.

Writing the Paragraph

The children were now ready to write their individual paragraphs. They had a list of words to use, a number of possible beginning sentences, and a few ways of ending their paragraphs.

The students had to select a beginning sentence. Then they were to write middle sentences telling how the snowman was built, and finally choose an ending sentence to fit the paragraph.

Bobby Thompson followed Mrs. English's instructions carefully. Which beginning sentence did he use? Which ending sentence? What words in his paragraph can you find in the list on **pages 54 and 55?**

A STRANGE CLOWN

Beginning Sentence: Yesterday my pals and I had a great time building a snowman. We rolled
Middle Sentences: the soft, flaky snow into two big balls and one small one. We piled them one on top of the other. We added two stones for eyes, and one for his nose.
Ending Sentence: After perching an old hat on his head, we were looking at a very funny figure.

Naming the Paragraph

Did you notice that Bobby named his paragraph? He called it "A Strange Clown" because he thought the snowman made an amusing figure. A paragraph is not complete without a good title. The students suggested the following titles for a paragraph about a snowman:

Our Own Snowman	Snow Art
Snow Sculpture	Fun in the Snow
Building a Snowman	A Funny Figure

CLASS ASSIGNMENT

A   Write a paragraph about building a snowman. Use some of the words in the list on pages 54 and 55.

B   Select a title for each of these paragraphs:

_____

What fun we had building a snow fort in our yard. My brother and I rolled the sparkling snow into big balls. For the walls, we beat the balls flat and piled them row upon row. On either side we stuck in a twig on which we placed a piece of cloth for a flag. We felt like real builders when we had finished our work.

_____

Did you ever try sliding down a hill without a sled? In our neighborhood we use heavy pieces of cardboard. Sitting on these, we sail down the hill in a flash. We can't steer these make-believe sleds, so the ride sometimes ends in a snowdrift.

C   The following words could be used in a paragraph telling about the fun you had playing hide-and-seek. Read them. Suggest beginning sentences, ending sentences, and titles. Then write a paragraph of your own. Follow the plan that Bobby used when he wrote about building a snowman.

WHO PLAY	*WHAT THEY DO*
children	hide
boys and girls	run
companions	scamper
neighbors	dash
comrades	hunt
pals	chase
WHERE THEY HIDE	*HOW THEY FEEL*
under the steps	excited
in the garage	happy
in the den	clever
on the porch	carefree
behind a tree	cunning
in a hammock	lively

STORIES ABOUT COLUMBUS

We have read many stories about Christopher Columbus. We remember him especially in October. Mrs. English suggested that the students write paragraphs about him.

"You know many things about Columbus," said Mrs. English. "A paragraph must tell about one thing, so you must first decide what your *topic* will be. You may write about Columbus as a boy, about his meeting with Queen Isabella, about his voyage to the New World, or about his return to Spain."

The class decided to write about the boy Columbus on the wharf at Genoa. They thought of words to describe the young Columbus, the things he did, and what he saw. A student wrote the suggested words on the chalkboard:

COLUMBUS	WHAT HE DID	WHAT HE SAW
small	played on the wharf	busy wharf
dark-haired	visited the wharf	ships sail away
Italian	gazed at the sea	white sailed vessels
thoughtful	listened to the sailors'	great ships unloading
interested	stories	goods
watchful	dreamed of future	trading of merchandise
courageous	voyages	

The next step was to make an outline for the story. This was placed on the board so that students could follow it in writing their paragraphs about Columbus.

COLUMBUS AT THE WHARF

Beginning Sentence: Where Columbus was
Middle Sentences: What he did and what he saw
Ending Sentence: The last thing he saw, or
my personal reaction

Using the outline, one girl wrote a paragraph which she named "A Future Seaman":

	A FUTURE SEAMAN
Beginning Sentence:	When Christopher Columbus was a little boy, he enjoyed visiting the wharf at Genoa. He often gazed at the
Middle Sentences:	big ships as they sailed into the harbor. He would watch the strong sailors unload their precious cargoes. Is it any wonder that this young Italian boy
Ending Sentence:	dreamed of future sea voyages?

CLASS ASSIGNMENT

A   Answer the following questions about the paragraph, "A Future Seaman":

1   Did the writer use words suggested by the class?
2   Do the sentences develop the outline?
3   Which are the middle sentences? What do they tell about Columbus?
4   Does the ending sentence tell one more fact, or what the writer thought about her topic?
5   Does the title fit the paragraph? Is it a good one?

B   Name the nouns in the following paragraph:

AN OCEAN PLAYGROUND

Do you know where Columbus spent many pleasant days when he was a boy? He visited the old wooden wharf in Genoa. There he watched large ships sail in and out of the busy harbor. Sometimes he played on the sun-warmed decks of idle ships. No wonder this thoughtful lad became a great sailor!

C Write a paragraph on any one of these topics:

Columbus at Home   Columbus Aboard the
Columbus and Queen Isabella   Santa Maria
The Landing of Columbus   The Return to Spain
    in America   The Death of Columbus

D Below are two paragraphs written from an outline. Which
paragraph do you prefer?

BOOKS

Beginnning Sentence: A comparison of a book to something else

Middle Sentences: a.   Where it takes me
                      b.   Whom I meet
                      c.   What I learn

Ending Sentence: My reaction

AN AIRPLANE TRIP

To me, a book is like an airplane. I step aboard and soar
through the air to distant lands. I mingle with strange
people and listen to the brave deeds of heroes. I wish I
could be brave like them.

A MAGIC KEY

A book is like a magic key. It unlocks secret doors,
permitting me to enter the wondrous land of make-
believe. I see beautiful women riding strong white horses.
I come face to face with men with long silvery beards. I
never want to lose my magic key.

CHORAL SPEAKING

Before beginning to recite a poem, we must practice exercises to make our voices clear and strong. We must improve
our breathing, articulation and enunciation.

TUNING-UP EXERCISES

Breathing:

Breathe in deeply. Keep your shoulders and chest still. Exhale slowly through your nose. Repeat several times.

Enunciation:

Learn to use your lips and tongue in speaking. Hold a mirror before your mouth sometime and say something. Do you think your lips are lazy? See how they work when you pronounce all your words carefully and distinctly.

Practice saying this poem. Be attentive to vowel and consonant sounds, so that your words are spoken clearly and your voices sound pleasing.

THE SQUIRREL

Whisky, frisky,
Hippity hop.
Up he goes
To the tree top!

Whirly, twirly,
Round and round,
Down he scampers
To the ground.

Furly, curly,
What a tail!
Tall as a feather,
Broad as a sail!

Where's his supper?
In his shell,
Snappity, crackity,
Out it fell!
    –Unknown

"The Strangers"

Have any of you ever heard of unicorns? They are animals talked about in myths and legends. A unicorn looked like a delicate white horse, except it had a long, slender, twisted horn in the middle of its forehead. Its eyes were blue.

Although it was hard to capture unicorns, they were known for their gentleness. They were thought of as playful, wise, loving, and peaceful. It was said that their horns had magical powers.

Imagine looking out your window early one morning, when everyone else is asleep, and seeing four of these lovely animals. That experience is what this poem is about. Let us read it together. Try to have your voices express the wonder and excitement that was felt by the poet.

THE STRANGERS
by Audrey Alexandra Brown

Early this morning,
  About the break of day,
Hoofbeats came clashing
  Along the narrow way—

And I looked from my window
  And saw in the square
Four white unicorns
  Stepping pair by pair.

Dappled and clouded,
  So daintily they trod
On small hoofs of ivory
  Silver-shod.

Tameless but gentle,
  Wondering yet wise,
They stared from their silver-lashed
  Sea-blue eyes.

The street was empty
  And blind with dawn—
The shutters were fastened,
  The bolts were drawn,

And sleepers half-rousing
  Said with a sigh,
"There goes the milk,"
  As the hoofs went by!

Answer these questions on "The Strangers":

1 What is the "square" in the poem?
2 Why does the poet say the unicorns were "dappled and clouded"?·
3 What are "shutters"?
4 Other people in the town heard the unicorns' hoofbeats. What did they think they were hearing?

CHAPTER FOUR Painting Word Pictures

The children thought this poem expressed their feelings about springtime.

SPRING
by Karla Kuskin

I'm shouting
I'm singing
I'm swinging through trees
I'm winging skyhigh
With the buzzing black bees.
I'm the sun
I'm the moon
I'm the dew on the rose.
I'm a rabbit
Whose habit
Is twitching his nose.
I'm lively
I'm lovely
I'm kicking my heels.
I'm crying "Come dance"
To the fresh water eels.
I'm racing through meadows
Without any coat
I'm a gamboling lamb
I'm a light leaping goat
I'm a bud
I'm a bloom
I'm a dove on the wing.
I'm running on rooftops
And welcoming spring!

CLASS ASSIGNMENT

A   Name any picture words in the poem "Spring."
B   Have a class talk on the special pleasures that you have discovered about springtime.

WRITING PARAGRAPHS ABOUT SPRING

Because nature is so beautiful in the spring, we like to
write paragraphs telling of the many changes we see. The
twins and their classmates liked spring flowers best. Each
student wrote a paragraph about his or her favorite spring
flower.

They made a list of the names of spring flowers, their
colors, their appearances, their growing places, and their
fragrances.

NAMES OF FLOWERS	COLORS	APPEARANCES
violets	purple	dainty
buttercups	golden	colorful
tulips	blue	stately
lilacs	red	tall
daffodils	yellow	upright

GROWING PLACES	FRAGRANCES
woods	sweet-smelling
gardens	delicate
back yards	heavily perfumed
valleys	spicy
lawns	rose-scented

The following outline helped the students write their own paragraphs:

MY FAVORITE FLOWER

Beginning Sentence:	My favorite flower
Middle Sentences:	Where it grows
	How it smells
Ending Sentence:	My feelings

Mrs. English asked the children to suggest some good beginning sentences for paragraphs about spring flowers. Do these sentences make good beginnings? Do they give a hint of what the paragraph is about?

1 The dainty violet is one of the prettiest of wild flowers.
2 One of the first signs of spring is the bright yellow buttercup.
3 Tulips of every color are seen in early spring.
4 My favorite flowers are the golden daffodils.

In the ending sentence, the children were to express their feelings about their favorite spring flower. The following ending sentences were suggested by the twins' classmates:

1 The modest violet has always been my favorite flower.
2 Of all the wild flowers, I like the buttercup best.
3 What a beautiful picture our garden of tulips makes in the spring!
4 My bed of daffodils is like a splash of golden sunshine.

A paragraph is not finished until it has been named. These titles were suggested by the students:

Spring's Gift	My Favorite Flower	Spring Blossoms
My Choice	Signs of Spring	Tulip-Talk

The following paragraph was written by one girl. Did she follow the outline?

MODEL: MY FAVORITE SPRING FLOWER

The dainty violet is one of the prettiest of wild flowers. Early in the spring it is seen in shady valleys and along riverbanks. The gentle breeze carries the delicate fragrance of its deep purple blossoms. Violets have always been my favorite flowers.

USING ADJECTIVES

We have learned how to make our sentences better by using descriptive words to color them. After we have written a paragraph, we should read each sentence carefully. We should try to improve the sentences by changing plain words to picture words or by adding picture words. Examine the changes made in the following sentences.

FIRST WRITING	PICTURE SENTENCES
The blossoms moved in the breeze.	The blossoms *swayed* in the breeze.
The tree was heavy with blossoms.	The *apple* tree was heavy with *delicate, pink* blossoms.

Russ wrote a paragraph about wild flowers. When he had finished, he made the paragraph better by adding adjectives or picture words. Can you find the improvements which he made?

SPRING FLOWERS

I like the wild flowers that bloom in the springtime. Buttercups grow along roadsides and riverbanks. In the forest, violets are close to the ground. To me, wild flowers are the jewels of spring.

SPRING'S JEWELS

I like the colorful wild flowers that bloom in the gentle springtime. Glossy yellow buttercups fill the roadsides and the riverbanks. In the shady forest, dainty violets nestle close to the soft earth. To me, wild flowers are the beautiful jewels of spring.

Which of Russ's paragraphs paints a clearer picture. Which title do you prefer?

Terry wrote a paragraph about violets. Mrs. English asked him to read it to the class. She said, "Terry, you did not follow the outline. Your middle sentences do not tell us about the flowers. We like your paragraph because your thoughts are beautiful."

Here is Terry's paragraph about violets.

MOTHER'S FRIENDS ARE MY FRIENDS

Can you guess why I like violets so much? It is because my mother likes them. When I pick these dainty flowers in the woods for her, she is happy. Violets are my friends because they are her favorites, too.

CLASS ASSIGNMENT

A   Write a beginning sentence for this paragraph:

A LOVELY BUSH

_____ . They bloom on leafy bushes in early spring. The fragrance of the cone-shaped flowers fills the air with sweet perfume. I think beautiful purple lilacs are spring's loveliest flowers.

B   Improve this paragraph by using in each blank space a picture word from the list below.

TULIPS

_____ tulips are blooming in our _____ garden. These _____ flowers look like bells and they have _____ green leaves. _____ red, _____ white, _____ yellow, and _____ purple are some of their colors. The _____ tulip is my favorite flower.

pretty	broad	dark
sunny	fiery	colorful
graceful	snowy	beautiful
flower	bright	golden

C   Supply a good ending sentence, and select an attractive title for the following paragraph:

_____

   The golden daffodils are my favorite spring flowers. They often grow beside sparkling lakes, and sometimes beneath budding trees. Standing upright, they resemble soldiers on parade. _____
_____ .

D   Write a paragraph about your favorite spring flower. Use adjectives to make a clear picture.

CHANGING WEAK WORDS TO STRONG WORDS

Our paragraphs and rhymes will be more interesting when we use strong words wherever possible. Study these sentences:

> The lion *walked* through the jungle.
> The lion *prowled* through the jungle.

Both the words *walked* and *prowled* tell what the lion did, but the word *prowled* gives a better picture of *how* he walked through the jungle. We call *prowled* a strong word.

Which of these sentences paints the better picture? Name the strong word.

> A chipmunk *ran* across the grass.
> A chipmunk *scampered* across the grass.

Action puts life into pictures, and so our sentences must express action. Choosing the correct verb is one way to bring words to life. Study the effects of action words in the following sentences:

1   The boy *came* down the street.
2   The boy *dashed* down the street.
        raced
        rushed
        skipped
        sauntered

1   The wind *blew*.
2   The wind *shrieked*.
        moaned.
        howled.
        screamed.
        roared.

1   Over the rails *went* the train.
2   Over the rails *thundered* the train.
        screeched
        rumbled
        sped

Can you see the difference in a sentence when the correct verbs are used? Improve your writing in this way. The exercises that follow should help.

CLASS ASSIGNMENT

A   Use these sentences for class discussion. Tell what words have been added to the plain sentences in the left-hand column to make the sentences in the right-hand column. Concentrate on verbs and vivid adjectives.

PLAIN SENTENCES	VIVID SENTENCES
1 The little children laughed.	The happy little children laughed merrily.
2 Vincent whistled a tune.	Vincent whistled a cheery tune.
3 We heard a sound at the door.	We heard a faint scratching sound at the tightly closed door.
4 The moon was rising in the sky.	The round, golden moon was rising in the cloudless sky.
5 The boys coasted down the hill.	The laughing boys coasted down the steep hill.
6 Columbus was a sailor.	Columbus was a brave Italian Sailor.
7 There were two pillows on my bed.	There were two huge feather pillows on my wide bed.
8 The train rushed along the rails.	The express train rushed along the shining rails.
9 The boy rode down the street.	The messenger boy rode down the narrow street.
10 Do you like the colors of the leaves?	Do you like the bright colors of the autumn leaves?
11 The rabbit ate the lettuce leaves.	The rabbit nibbled the lettuce leaves.
12 The canoe went across the lake.	The canoe glided across the lake.
13 The baby walked across the floor.	The baby toddled across the floor.
14 Our snow fort fell down.	Our snow fort collapsed.
15 The dog made a noise.	The dog growled.
16 The boys went into the swimming pool.	The boys plunged into the swimming pool.

B Copy the following sentences. In each sentence change the word or words printed in italics to the word in parentheses.

  1 His eyes *looked angry*. (blazed)
  2 He *threw* the rock into the stream. (hurled)
  3 The clouds *moved* across the sky. (floated)
  4 The waves *came* up to the shore. (dashed)
  5 Fluffy *pulled* at the tablecloth. (tugged)
  6 We *walked* down the lane. (strolled)
  7 The old man *moved* across the room. (shuffled)
  8 Moonbeams *were shining* on the lake. (danced)

C Copy these sentences. Add adjectives, descriptive words in the blank spaces:

  1 I have a _____ ball.
  2 The _____ butterfly drifted away.
  3 There is a _____ bridge over the _____ river.
  4 The _____ boy crept down the _____ stairs.
  5 _____ ships made their way into the _____ harbor.
  6 Five _____ kittens lay in the _____ basket.
  7 Did your mother bake this _____ pie?
  8 The _____ wind blew.
  9 The _____ dog was barking at the _____ man.
  10 _____ flowers grew near the _____ house.
  11 What a _____ puppy you have!
  12 The _____ birds flew to the top of the _____ tree.
  13 Robert is wearing his _____ suit.
  14 "What a _____ palace!" said the _____ princess.
  15 Do you ever read _____ stories about children in _____ lands?
  16 My _____ grandmother gave me a game for my birthday.

POLISHING SENTENCES

Our sentences can be greatly improved by substituting adjectives and strong action words for dull and overworked words. We may also find that some of our sentences require more than a change of words.

Adding Colorful Pictures and Comparisons

Good writers create vivid pictures in their sentences. They do this by using comparisons or similes.

Anything may be described by comparing it with something else. If you want to tell someone that your new curtains are made of thin material, you might say that the material is "as thin as a butterfly's wing." Something round could be explained by saying that it is "as round as a button."

Tissue paper is as thin as a butterfly's wing.

My baby brother's nose looks as round as a button.

Study the comparisons in these sentences:

The stars look like little electric lights.
The new moon is like a piece of honeydew melon.
My kitten is like a ball of white fur.

stars–electric lights   moon–piece of melon   kitten– ball of white fur

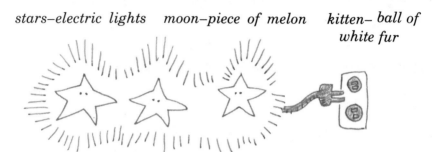

When we make a comparison, we tell how one thing is said to be *like* or *as* another. Comparisons help make sentences clear and vivid.

CLASS ASSIGNMENT

A   Select from the list below a word that can be used to compare the two things mentioned in each sentence.

| smooth | soft | straight |
| rough | hard | crooked |

1   The ice was as _____ as a sheet of glass.
2   This frozen ice cream feels as _____ as a rock.
3   My baby sister's hair is as_____ as cotton.
4   The soldier stood as _____ as a yardstick.
5   My father's whiskers feel like_____ sandpaper.
6   Mark drew lines as _____ as a winding path.

B   Think of a word which names something you could compare with each of the following expressions.

1   as wet as falling rain   4   as squirmy as a caterpiller
2   as dry as potato chips   5   as tall as an oak
3   as loud as a firecracker.   6   as small as an ant

Combining Short Sentences

Many of the sentences we write are short and choppy. Paragraphs can be improved by combining two or more short sentences. This is done by placing *and* or some other connecting words, between the two sentences. Other words that may be used are *but, when, where, as, who, although, which,* and *because.*

SHORT SENTENCES	COMBINED SENTENCES
I hurried this morning. I missed the school bus.	I hurried this morning, *but* I missed the school bus.
I crossed the ocean. I was six years old.	*When* I was six years old, I crossed the ocean.

CLASS ASSIGNMENT

Combine these short sentences, using a connecting word such as those given above:

1 Gerald cut the grass. He was tired.
2 Maria fed the birds. She ate her breakfast.
3 It was Saturday. Michael weeded the garden.
4 We were playing ball. Spot took the ball.
5 Janet will be the leader. We will follow.
6 We finished our work. We went ice skating.
7 I did not know the way. I arrived early.
8 The mail carrier left the letters. He did not leave a package.
9 The squad obeyed promptly. The leader gave the command.
10 Alice draws well. Her penmanship is poor.

POLISHING THE PARAGRAPH

Now that we have learned to improve words and sentences, we must apply all these methods to the paragraphs we write. See how other students have improved their paragraphs.

First Draft
A WINDY DAY

One day the wind played with me. He took my cap just as I got to the corner. He ran down the street with it. When I ran after him, he put my hat under a bush. The wind likes to play.

Improved Draft
A TEASING WIND

One blustery day that old wind played a game with me. Just as I reached the corner of our street, he snatched my bright red cap. Down the street he raced with it. When I dashed after it, he threw it under an evergreen bush. I guess the wind likes to play as much as children do.

First Draft
A GAME

My friends and I played a game yesterday. Some of the children went up the alley, followed by their companions. Other children ran under the steps. One boy hid in the bushes. We were all happy playing this game.

Improved Draft
HIDE-AND-SEEK FUN

My friends and I played a great game of hide-and-seek yesterday after school. Some of the children dashed up the alley, chased by their happy companions. Other boys and girls scampered under the steps. One clever boy hid in the bushes. We all enjoyed the time spent playing this carefree game.

CLASS ASSIGNMENT

A This paragraph has been improved. Tell how this was done.

First Draft	Improved Draft
A BICYCLE	*A PRIZED GIFT*
My new bicycle is nice. A maroon coat covers its steel body. The bars and the spokes are painted. It has a nice leather seat and cushion tires. I hope people see it when I ride through the streets.	*My new bicycle is a beauty. A maroon coat of paint covers its steel body. The handlebars and wheel spokes are tan. It has a fine leather seat and cushion tires. How proud I shall be to ride it through the streets!*

B Improve the first draft of this paragraph:

My heart beat as I saw the silver plane at the airport. Soon we were on it and away we went. In no time we were above the clouds. I was not scared, although I made sure to remain near my father.

POEMS AS WORD PICTURES

We can use word pictures in another way. A poem is a word picture. It puts into words what we see and hear all around us. Try to see the picture that this poem describes. Why is the poem pleasing to the ear?

WINTER DRESS

The snow tiptoes to earth;
It whispers its way down.
Then soon a robe of ermine
Becomes the world's new gown.

What picture does the poem paint? What words tell you that the snow falls silently? "The world's new gown" is what color? How do you know?

Rhyme contributes to the music in the poem, making it more pleasing to the ear. Name the two rhyming words in this poem. Can you think of three other words that rhyme with *down?*

CLASS ASSIGNMENT

A   Name words that rhyme with each of the words listed below. Try to use some of them in a poem of your own.

white	cold	flake	sleigh
still	fall	drift	glide

B   Here is a poem whose author is unknown. It tells how we should act toward others. Find the rhyming words.

CHORAL SPEAKING

Before reciting our poems together, we will again have tuning-up exercises in breathing and enunciation. These exercises will help us to speak in unison and to pronounce every syllable crisply and distinctly.

TUNING-UP EXERCISES

Breathing:

Inhale, hold the breath for eight counts, then exhale slowly as if blowing out a number of candles one by one.

Enunciation:

Learn to enunciate, or "speak out," both vowels and consonants. Consonants should be enunciated crisply and accurately. Vowels should be said with the mouth round. Practice saying the vowels. Say all the vowels first in low pitch, slow time; then repeat in quick time, high pitch. Say these short sounds with relaxed tongue:

a as in tag (repeat several times):   rap, pad, hat, patch, tap
Pat sat on the mat.

e as in pet (repeat several times):   sell, fell, tell, ten, hen, men
Tell Nell to sell the bell.

Now that our voices are in tune, let us try reading this nonsense rhyme together.

ALLIGATOR PIE
by Dennis Lee

Alligator pie, alligator pie,
If I don't get some I think I'm gonna die.
Give away the green grass, give away the sky,
But don't give away my alligator pie.

Alligator stew, alligator stew,
If I don't get some I don't know what I'll do.
Give away my furry hat, give away my shoe,
But don't give away my alligator stew.

Alligator soup, alligator soup,
If I don't get some, I think I'm gonna droop.
Give away my hockey-stick, give away my hoop,
But don't give away my alligator soup.

Emma's Store

Christine brought a book of poems to school. She told her classmates about one poem she especially liked called "Emma's Store." It reminded her of an old store in the small town where her grandmother lives. Have you ever been in a nice, homey store like the one in the poem?

Let's read "Emma's Store" together. Those with deeper voices will read the first line, then those with lighter voices will read the second one. We will alternate lines that way to the end of the poem.

EMMA'S STORE
by Dorothy Aldis

Deeper Voices:	The store we like best is Emma's store.
Lighter Voices:	It hasn't any revolving door.
Deeper Voices:	It hasn't a floorman neat and polite:
Lighter Voices:	"Third floor, Modom, and turn to your right."
Deeper Voices:	No elevators go up and down it.
Lighter Voices:	Nothing's the way it is downtown. It
Deeper Voices:	Hasn't a special place for dresses;
Lighter Voices:	Everything's jumbled in cozy messes—
Deeper Voices:	Washcloths and lamp shades, paper dolls, slippers,
Lighter Voices:	Candy and shoestrings, umbrellas and zippers;
Deeper Voices:	No matter what's needed or how great the hurry
Lighter Voices:	As long as there's Emma's, you don't need to worry.
Deeper Voices:	And *she* never minds how long you stay.
Lighter Voices:	"Why sure, take your time, dear," Emma will say.

CHAPTER FIVE Celebrating Holidays

$\mathbb{S}$usan and Steve liked November and December because there were so many holidays to be celebrated.

PLANNING PROGRAMS

First came Veterans Day, or Remembrance Day as it is known in Canada. On this day the children thought of all the brave soldiers, sailors, and airmen who died for their country. They planned a patriotic program to honor these friends.

At a discussion, with Mrs. English as leader, the children of the class planned this program:

1 Opening: singing of a patriotic song.
2 A short talk on a patriotic topic (meaning of Veterans Day).
3 Recitation of a patriotic poem.
4 Pledge of Allegiance to the flag.
5 Singing of the National Anthem.

Like children the world over, Susan and Steve were proud that they were loyal young citizens. They knew many stories about the brave men and women who had helped make their country great. They recited the Pledge of Allegiance to the flag each day in the classroom.

Every child in the United States should know these words:

I pledge Allegiance to the flag of the United States of America and to the republic for which it stands; one nation under God, indivisible, with liberty and justice for all.

Canadian children honor their country by singing the Canadian national anthem, "O Canada." This song tells of the glories of Canada with its great prairies and rivers.

CLASS ASSIGNMENT

Talk about Veterans Day, or Remembrance Day, in your classroom. Ask your teacher to help you plan a patriotic program showing that you are proud of your country. Do you know any patriotic songs? Children in the United States could sing "The Star-Spangled Banner," "America," "Columbia, the Gem of the Ocean," or "America the Beautiful." They could also recite a poem about the flag. At the end of the program, everyone should show his or her love of country by pledging allegiance to the flag.

Canadian children might close their program by singing "O Canada."

WRITING LETTERS

National holidays are not the only days we celebrate. There are special family days, such as birthdays, weddings, anniversaries, graduations, and so forth, which we share with our families and friends. Do you remember Susan and Steve's birthday? They called some of their friends by telephone and invited them to their party. They also wrote letters to friends they could not reach by phone. We all like to receive letters. Writing letters is how we keep in touch. They are little messengers carrying our thoughts to far-away places. In this chapter we will study letters. You will learn to write different kinds of letters so that you can share special days and important events with others.

Letters of Invitation

Susan wrote this invitation on white letter paper, using black ink. She wrote neatly and clearly:

Dear Bob,

Mother and Father say that we may have a party in honor of our eighth birthday. It will be held at our home on Saturday, October 17, from two until five o'clock. Will you be one of our guests?

Your friends,

Steve and Susan Parker

The Parts of a Letter

The first line of Susan's letter is called the greeting or *salutation*. Had Susan met Bob, she would have greeted him by saying, "Hello, Bob." In writing letters, we greet our friends by expressions like "Dear Bob," or "Dear Jane."

After the greeting, Susan wrote her message. This part of a letter is called the *body*. In an invitation, we must tell what the occasion is: a party, a picnic, a play, a football game, or a day at the beach. We must also tell the place, the date, and the time of the event.

Susan now wanted to say "Good-bye." She wrote "Your friends" on the line after the body. This part of the letter is called the *closing*.

Susan signed Steve's name and her own after the closing. The part of the letter where the writer signs his or her name is called the *signature*.

Learn the names of these four parts of a letter: the *salutation*, the *body*, the *closing*, and the *signature*. Each part, except the body, contains one line.

Arranging the Letter on Paper

Susan wrote the salutation near the top of the paper, leaving about half an inch to the left. We should leave some space at the top, the bottom, and on the left and right sides. These are *margins*.

Susan wrote *Dear* and *Bob* with capital letters. She placed a comma after the salutation. She began the first word of the body under *Bob*. She *indented* it. This means that she moved it in a little from the left-hand margin. All the other sentences in the body of the letter began under the word *Dear*. We should be careful to keep the left-hand margin even. We leave a space on the right side of the paper. Our right-hand margins should be as even as possible.

After we finish writing the body of a letter, we write the closing on the line following. The first word of the closing begins at about the middle of the paper from left to right. The *first word* begins with a capital letter, and is followed by a comma. Susan used the word *friends* in the closing of her letter because she and Steve were twins, and the party was for both of them. If one person gave a party, he would say "Your friend." If he invited his cousin, he would probably write "Your cousin," as Rich did on page 92.

The signature is written under the *first word* of the closing. If we are writing to relatives or close friends, we use only our first name. If we are writing to someone who does not know us very well, we use both our first and last names.

CLASS ASSIGNMENT

A   Name the four parts of a letter. Tell what each part contains.

B   Copy this invitation. Use pen and ink, keep the left-hand margin even, and be sure to write the commas, periods, and capital letters correctly.

Dear Ed,
   Saturday, September 15, is my birthday. Mother is giving a party for me at our home. It will begin at three o'clock. I should like very much to have you come.

                        Your cousin,
                           Rich

C   Pretend you are having a birthday party at your aunt's house on Thursday, October 1, at four o'clock. Write a letter inviting one of your friends.

D   Your brother is going away to boarding school. On the day before he leaves, your mother is planning a surprise party in his honor. Invite one of his friends to this party. Be sure to mention that it is a surprise and that your brother does not know about it.

SAYING "THANK YOU"

One day the students in the class were talking about birthdays. Mrs. English asked them if they always thanked the people who gave them presents. Susan told the class about the presents that she and Steve had received at their party. She said they both thanked the children for the gifts. Steve told Mrs. English that they telephoned their Uncle Thomas to thank him for the roller skates, and wrote a letter thanking their grandmother for a book.

One girl in the class said that she had received a present from her Aunt Laura who lived in another city, but she did not know how to write a letter that would say "Thank you."

The teacher explained that a thank-you letter has the same parts as a letter of invitation—the salutation, body, closing, and signature.

In the body of the letter, Jill should thank her Aunt Laura for the gift. There are three special things that we must do in a thank-you letter. These are shown in the box on this page.

> **In a Thank-You Letter:**
> *1 We say "Thank you."*
> *2 We name the gift.*
> *3 We tell why we like it, or how we used it.*

"What did your aunt send you, Jill, and why do you like it?" asked Mrs. English. Jill said that her aunt had sent her a pair of red and white mittens, and she liked them because they kept her hands warm. "Then you should thank your aunt for the mittens and tell her that you like them because they keep you warm," said Mrs. English. "I will write the letter of thanks on the chalkboard."

94

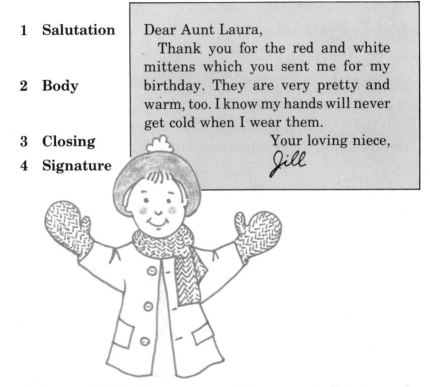

1	Salutation	Dear Aunt Laura,
2	Body	Thank you for the red and white mittens which you sent me for my birthday. They are very pretty and warm, too. I know my hands will never get cold when I wear them.
3	Closing	Your loving niece,
4	Signature	Jill

Jill copied this letter and sent it to her aunt. Point out the salutation, the closing, and the signature in the letter.

CLASS ASSIGNMENT

Read this letter, and then answer the questions that follow:

Dear Uncle Salvador,

What a surprise I received when I opened my birthday gift from you! The skates were just what I wanted. I can hardly wait until the pond is frozen, so that I can use them. Thank you, Uncle Salvador, for the happiness you have given me.

Your grateful nephew,

Julio

1   Did Julio say "Thank you"?
2   Did his letter mention what the gift was?
3   Did he tell why he liked the present?
4   What do we call the part of the letter that says "Dear Uncle Salvador"?
5   What is the word "Julio" called?
6   What is the part above Julio's name called?

The Salutation of a Letter

The *salutation* of a letter is a greeting. It states to whom we are writing the letter. Jill used the greeting "Dear Aunt Laura" in her letter to her aunt. The twins used the salutation "Dear Bob" when they wrote their invitation.

The first word of the salutation and the name of the person to whom we are writing begin with capital letters. The word *dear* does not begin with a capital letter unless it is the *first word* of the salutation. We place a comma after the salutation.

The kind of greeting we use depends upon the person to whom we are writing. Here are some of the salutations we might use in our letters:

FOR RELATIVES

Dear Father,
Mother dear,
My dear Grandparents,
Dear Cousin Otto,

FOR FRIENDS

Dear Jerome,
Dearest friend,
Dear Barbara,
Dear Mrs. Dacey,

Review the lesson on the salutation by reciting the following jingle:

> The salutation says hello;
> And since good form you wish to show,
> Capitalize the person's name,
> And then the first word—just the same.
> Now a comma you must place
> To show there is a definite space
> Between the friendly salutation
> And the following information.

CLASS ASSIGNMENT

A What salutation would you use in a letter to each of the following persons?

1	Your mother	4	A classmate
2	A cousin	5	Your father
3	Your teacher	6	Your Aunt Mary

B Copy George's thank-you letter and correct all the mistakes:

dear Aunt bertha

the book you sent me is very exciting   how did you know I like to read about Indians   the colored pictures help me to understand the story   thank you very much for this interesting book

your nephew

george

C Write a thank-you letter, using any one of these beginning sentences:

1 Thank you very much for the new sled, Grandfather.
2 The pretty doll you sent me for my birthday has made me very happy.
3 I love the little puppy you sent me for my birthday!
4 Of all my presents, the one I like best is the wrist watch that you sent me.
5 At last I have a bicycle of my own!

The Closing of a Letter

After we have written the message, we say good-bye in the closing. Susan used the closing "Your loving child" when she wrote a letter to her parents. Carlos wrote "Your loving son" in his letter. In a thank-you letter we might say "Your loving granddaughter" if we are writing to our grandparents or "Your grateful nephew" if we are writing to an aunt or an uncle.

Here are some closings that could be used for different persons:

FOR RELATIVES	FOR FRIENDS
Your loving son,	Your student,
Your grateful daughter,	Your loving friend,
Your devoted grandson,	Your classmate,
Your affectionate cousin,	Your old pal,
Your nephew,	Your buddy,

We begin to write the closing of a letter a little to the right of the center of the paper on the line below the body. Only the first word of the closing begins with a capital letter. A comma is placed after the closing.

The following jingle will help you remember how to write the closing of a letter:

A capital letter always goes
To start the complimentary close.
And with a comma at the end
You say "good-bye" to your friend.

LETTERS ABOUT GAMES

A few days after the students had given talks about outdoor sports, Mrs. English asked them to write a letter about a game. She explained that they could write to a friend or relative in another city, telling about a game they enjoyed.

Anne Vaughn wrote the following letter to a classmate who had moved away:

Dear Margaret,

We learned a new game in school since you moved to Kansas City. It is called "pantomime." We pretend that we are doing something, and the others guess from our motions and the expressions on our faces what it is. No words are spoken at all. We like pantomimes very much. Please write and tell me if you would enjoy playing this game.

Your friend,

Anne Vaughn

Saying "Please"

When Anne read her letter to the class, Mrs. English praised her because she said "Please write" and not just "Write." A polite person always says "Please" when asking someone to do something for him or her.

To teach the students to say "Please," Mrs. English wrote a poem on the chalkboard. The children did not soon forget the lesson it taught.

THE LITTLE GIRL WHO WOULDN'T SAY PLEASE

There was once a small child who would never say please,
I believe, if you even went down on your knees.
But, her arms on the table, would sit at her ease,
And call out to her mother in words such as these:
"I want some potatoes!" "Give me some peas!"
"Hand me the butter!" "Cut me some cheese!"
So the fairies, this very rude daughter to tease,
Once blew her away in a powerful breeze,
Over the mountains, and over the seas,
To the valley where never a dinner she sees,
But down with the ants, the wasps, and the bees,
In the woods she must live till she learns to say please.

M.S.P.

Would your class like to learn this poem and recite it together? Appoint one child to say the words of the little girl in the story.

The Signature

Did you notice that Anne signed both her first name and her last name? She did this because she knew that Margaret had another friend whose name was Anne, and she wanted Margaret to know which Anne was writing.

When we are writing to our mother or father, or to anyone who knows us, we sign only our first name. When there is any doubt, sign first and last names.

The following jingle may help you remember about the signature:

> The signature is simply when
> You pause a moment with your pen,
> Then sign the letter with your name,
> Letting neatness be your aim.

CLASS ASSIGNMENT

A   What is the salutation in Anne's letter?
What closing did she use?
Why did Anne sign her last name?

B   Write a letter to a cousin or to a friend telling about a game that you enjoy playing.

C   Copy this letter written by Tony Martino. Be sure that all the parts of the letter are in the proper places:

Dear Art, Some of the boys in our neighborhood are going to hold a skating contest in Lincoln Park on Saturday afternoon, March 5, at two o'clock. Don't forget to come. You might be the new champion! Your friend, Tony Martino

---

SHARING OUR PLEASURES

One day the class gave a play during the story hour. When the program was over, Barbara said "I have often read the story of the country mouse and the city mouse to my little brother in second grade. I wish he could see our play."

Mrs. English replied that the club could decide about repeating the program and inviting the second grade. As chairman of the meeting, Jerome asked the members to vote. All the children were in favor of the suggestion made by Barbara.

Mrs. English helped the children write a letter of invitation to the second grade. In this letter they used a part not studied before. It is called the *heading*.

Writing the Heading

The *heading* of a letter consists of three lines. On the first line we write our street address. If we write a letter from school, as these children did, we use the name of our school instead of our own address. On the second line we write the name of the city, the name of the state or province, and the zip code number. We place a comma after the name of the city. On the third line we write the date: the month, day, and year. We place a comma between the day of the month and the year.

Every word in the heading of a letter begins with a capital letter. We know that the name of a school begins with a capital letter. The names of streets, cities, states, provinces, and months also begin with capital letters.

The first line of the heading should be written about an inch down from the top of the paper and a little to the right of the center. The first word of the second line and the first word of the third line are written directly under the first word of the first line.

The Scott Elementary School
Providence, Rhode Island 02906
February 4, 19___

Dear Second Grade,

Some people from "Story Land" will be in our classroom on Friday, February 10, at three o'clock, when our Story Tellers Club meets. We want you to share the fun with us. Please be our guests.

Your friends,
Room 43

CLASS ASSIGNMENT

A   When you copy this heading, place a comma between the name of the city and the state, and a comma between the day of the month and the year:

1520 Davis Street
Evanston Illinois 60201
May 7 19___

B   Copy the following heading. Use capital letters where they are needed.

830 main street
honolulu, hawaii 96818
april 24, 19___

C   Write the following in heading form for a letter:

150 Court Street, Montreal, H3B 3J3 Quebec, March 12, 19___

D   Correct the mistakes as you copy the following letter:

robert e. lee school
milwaukee, wisconsin 53207
March 24, 19__

dear second grade,

at three o'clock on Friday afternoon, March 28, we
are going to have a story hour in our classroom. We
would like to have you hear our tales about animals.
will you come?

your friends,
Room 13

A LETTER FOR STUDY AND EXAMINATION

Heading	112 Donnelly Avenue Green Ridge, PA 19014 October 15, 19__
Salutation	Dear Jim, Our favorite game at school now is baseball. Every afternoon after class we take our bat and ball to the schoolyard and play. Our team, the Red Stars, has won many games. Please write and tell me if you have a
Body	baseball team at your school.
Closing	Your cousin,
Signature	*Patrick*

Do you know the answers to these questions?

1 What is the heading of this letter?
2 How many commas are in the heading? Where are they placed?
3 All words in the heading begin with _____ letters.
4 What is the salutation?
5 The mark of punctuation following the salutation is a _____ .
6 What is contained in the body of this letter?
7 How many sentences are in the body?
8 What is the closing of this letter?
9 What word in the closing begins with a capital letter?
10 What mark of punctuation follows the closing?
11 What is the signature?
12 Why is Patrick's last name not written in his letter?

WHEN OUR PETS CAUSE TROUBLE

One morning Mrs. English noticed that Raphael seemed very unhappy. When she asked why, he said that the man who lived next door was angry because Raphael's rabbit had entered his garden. "Mr. Bannon says he's going to shoot Cotton the next time he eats his carrots," sobbed Raphael.

"Pets often cause trouble between neighbors," said Mrs. English. "Don't you think your neighbor might forgive Cotton if you wrote him a little letter saying how sorry you are? Your classmates will be glad to help you. They probably have had trouble with pets, too."

"My cat once chased our neighbor's bird," said Judy. "Mother told me to go to Mrs. Watson's house and tell her I was sorry for what my cat did. Mrs. Watson was very kind when I talked to her. Smog rarely ever chased her bird again."

This is the letter to Mr. Bannon that Raphael wrote with the help of his classmates:

8222 Michener Avenue
Philadelphia, PA 19138
May 11, 19___

Dear Mr. Bannon,

I am very sorry that Cotton ate some of your carrots yesterday. Rabbits like carrots, and they cannot help eating them when they get into a garden. I shall be glad to plant more carrots for you on Saturday. The wire on Cotton's home has been fixed, and I hope he will not escape again.

Your neighbor,

Raphael

Addressing the Envelope

Raphael wanted to send the letter to Mr. Bannon through the mail. It was a good time for the children to learn how to address an envelope.

On an envelope we write the full name and address of the person to whom the letter is sent. We find the center of the envelope, then move our pen a little to the left and just above the center. Here we write the person's name. Below his name we write his address—the number of his house and the name of the street. On the next line we write the name of the city in which he lives, the abbreviation for the state, and the zip code. In the upper left-hand corner of the envelope we should write our own address.

This is the way Raphael addressed the envelope that he sent to Mr. Bannon:

```
8222 Michener Avenue                            ┌───┐
Philadelphia, PA 19138                          │   │
                                                └╌╌╌┘


                    Mr. Donald Bannon
                    8224 Michener Avenue
                    Philadelphia, PA 19138
```

Notice that Raphael used a capital letter to begin each word in Mr. Bannon's name, and in the names of the street, city, and state. He used a comma after the name of the city.

The following is a list of the two-letter state abbreviations which the United States Post Office expects us to use:

AL	Alabama	KY	Kentucky	ND	North Dakota
AK	Alaska	LA	Louisiana	OH	Ohio
AZ	Arizona	ME	Maine	OK	Oklahoma
AR	Arkansas	MD	Maryland	OR	Oregon
CA	California	MA	Massachusetts	PA	Pennsylvania
CO	Colorado	MI	Michigan	RI	Rhode Island
CT	Connecticut	MN	Minnesota	SC	South Carolina
DE	Delware	MS	Mississippi	SD	South Dakota
DC	District of	MO	Missouri	TN	Tennessee
	Columbia	MT	Montana	TX	Texas
FL	Florida	NE	Nebraska	UT	Utah
GA	Georgia	NV	Nevada	VT	Vermont
HI	Hawaii	NH	New Hampshire	VA	Virginia
ID	Idaho	NJ	New Jersey	WA	Washington
IL	Illinois	NM	New Mexico	WV	West Virginia
IN	Indiana	NY	New York	WI	Wisconsin
IA	Iowa	NC	North Carolina	WY	Wyoming
KS	Kansas				
		GU	Guam	VI	Virgin Islands
		PR	Puerto Rico		

CLASS ASSIGNMENT

A Draw rectangles on paper to represent envelopes. Write the following names and addresses as they should be written. Use your own address in the upper left-hand corner.

1 Miss Dorothy King, 423 West Sherbrook Street, Montreal, H4B 1R6 Quebec

2 Mr. Ambrose Gallagher, 914 Capitol Avenue, Cleveland, Ohio 44104

3 Mr. Anthony Kane, 600 Pennsylvania Avenue, Manila, Philippines

4 Mr. Wallace Young, 711 East Pine Street, Albany, New York 12207

5 Miss Marie Donnelly, 619 Warren Avenue, Dallas, Texas 75215

B Correct the mistakes on this envelope:

5503 Greenwood street
toledo, ohio 43612

dr denis sullivan
1140 North jefferson avenue
fort Wayne, indiana 46803

C Answer the following questions about Raphael's letter on page 105:

1 What is the heading of the letter?

2 What salutation did Raphael use?

3 What is the name of that part of the letter which says "Your neighbor"?

4 What does Raphael say in the body of his letter?

5 Where is his signature written?

6 What mark of punctuation is used after the salutation?

7 What punctuation mark follows the closing?

8 Why did Raphael sign only his first name?

D   Copy this letter written by Rose O'Brien. Be sure that all parts of the letter are written properly.

> 137 Lawton Avenue, Tulsa, Oklahoma, 74127, April 6, 19—
>
> Dear Mrs. Webster, I am sorry that your cat was frightened yesterday. We were having a party when Gemini came into the yard. Suddenly she began to tug at the tablecloth. Down came a pitcher of cream. I am sure Gemini did not expect to have her cream served in this manner. Your friend, Rose.

E   Address the envelope to Mrs. Webster, who lives at 139 Lawton Avenue, Tulsa, Oklahoma, 74127, using Rose's address in the upper left-hand corner.

WRITING A LETTER OF ACCEPTANCE

One day Mrs. English's students were very happy because they received an invitation from the fourth grade to attend a Book Fair. All wanted to answer and accept the invitation.

Mrs. English explained that a letter accepting an invitation is called a *letter of acceptance*. In such a letter we say "Thank you" for the invitation and tell how happy we are to come. We repeat the date, the hour, and the place, to show that we will not forget.

This is the letter the class wrote to their friends in fourth grade:

> Brooks Elementary School
> Philadelphia, PA   19138
> May 12, 19—
>
> Dear Fourth Grade,
>   Thank you for inviting us to your Book Fair on May 16. We like books very much. Promptly at two o'clock we will come to your room.
>
> Your friends,
> Room 13

CLASS ASSIGNMENT

A Answer these questions about the model letter of acceptance on page 108:
1 Did the third-grade children say "Thank you"?
2 On what date and at what hour is the Book Fair to be held?
3 Do you think the third-grade students were pleased to receive this invitation?

B Copy this letter of acceptance. Put in commas and periods where they are needed.

> Brocks Elementary School
> Kodiak Alaska 99615
> April 16 19__
>
> Dear Fourth Grade
> We shall be glad to come to the Story Tellers Club program on Tuesday April 26 at three o-clock Thank you for asking us We know that the stories you are going to tell will be very interesting to us
> Your friends
> *The Third Grade*

C Write a letter to the second grade accepting an invitation to a Memorial Day program.

A RIDE IN AN AIRPLANE

All the children in Steve and Susan's class had seen airplanes. They could imagine what it was like to fly high above the earth. Many of the children had visited airports and had been inside planes. They were very happy when Mrs. English told them to write letters about a make-believe airplane ride. Susan's letter is below:

---

809 High Street
Philadelphia, PA 19144
May 15, 19—

Dear Becky,

What a thrill Steve and I had last Sunday! Dad took us for our first airplane ride. We soared through the clouds in the large silver plane for more than an hour. The houses below looked like dolls' houses, and in the country the fields looked like a patchwork quilt. I think even the birds envied our sky ride.

Your friend,
Susan

CLASS ASSIGNMENT

A Copy Susan's letter on a sheet of letter paper.

B Copy this letter on a sheet of letter paper. Be sure to put each part in the proper place.

Dear Ralph, May 14, 19— , 530 East Fordham Road, Bronx, New York 10458   Last week, I took my first trip by air. At eight o'clock in the morning, the plane left New York. Dad and I were at my grandmother's home in Montreal by ten o'clock. I think traveling by air is the quickest way to go anywhere! Alan   Your pal,

C Insert missing parts when you copy this letter:

>Did you ever sail through the clouds in an airplane? I did last Saturday when Mother took me to Washington. High above the earth the plane flew like a giant bird. I will never forget that wonderful ride!

D Write a letter about a ride you have taken in an airplane, an automobile, a boat, a bus, or a train.

CHORAL SPEAKING

A good orchestra must have all the instruments in tune before it performs a symphony. Likewise, our human voices must be in tune before we are able to speak well together. For this purpose, we practice tuning-up exercises before reading a poem in unison.

TUNING-UP EXERCISES

Breathing:

Inhale through the mouth or the nose, filling your diaphragm, chest wall, and ribs with air. Then exhale slowly with the sound of *ah*.

Enunciation:

It is important to "speak out" both vowels and consonants. Vowels should be said with the mouth round. Consonants should be spoken both sharply and accurately. Repeat the following sentence, giving each consonant its correct sound and saying the words clearly:

>Would you, could you, won't you, then why don't you?

Pronounce the following words, giving full value to the consonants in each word:

just	left	around	sound
letter	little	cold	already
fold	found	half past	library

Here is a delightful short poem by Evelyn Beyer which should help us to pronounce our vowels and consonants distinctly. Think of the animals in the poem. Short poems are usually good for practice in making our voices sound like one voice.

JUMP OR JIGGLE
by Evelyn Beyer

Frogs jump
Caterpillars hump

Worms wiggle
Bugs jiggle

Rabbits hop
Horses clop

Snakes slide
Sea gulls glide

Mice creep
Deer leap

Puppies bounce
Kittens pounce

Lions stalk—
But—
I walk!

The class should read "Tiptoe" silently before saying the poem together. For fun, and for practice in putting expression into your voices, read the poem in the tone of voice marked before each few lines. Continue in one tone of voice until another is indicated, then change to that one.

TIPTOE

By Karla Kuskin

Normal Voice: Yesterday I skipped all day,
The day before I ran;
Hushed Voice: Today I'm going to tiptoe
Everywhere I can.
I'll tiptoe down the stairway.
I'll tiptoe through the door.
I'll tiptoe to the living room
Loud Voice: And give an awful roar.
Normal Voice: And my father, who is reading,
Will jump up from his chair
And mumble something silly like,
"I didn't see you there."
Hushed Voice: I'll tiptoe to my mother
And give a little cough,
And when she spins to see me,
Why, I'll softly tiptoe off.
I'll tiptoe through the meadows,
Over hills and yellow sands,
And when my toes get tired,
Then I'll tiptoe on my hands.

CHAPTER SIX # Visits to Bookland

Would you like to own a magic carpet that would carry you to any part of the world? Books can be such magic carpets. They take us to many colorful places. We can fly to Mexico, Denmark, China or almost anywhere, and meet interesting people who soon become our friends. Books make the years roll back. We can visit the lands of long ago, when knights and heroes lived. There we may meet giants or fire-breathing dragons. How much there is to explore through books!

Susan and Steve found an exciting story about a brave knight who killed a dragon. They wanted their friends to read the story, too. Then they could talk about the wonderful deeds of the hero. Other children had books to share, so the students asked to build a mini-library in their classroom.

A CLASSROOM BOOK CORNER

Mrs. English was pleased that the children were so thoughtful, and that they were willing to share the books

they liked. She assigned a part of the classroom for a Book Corner. Everyone who had good books at home brought them in for the classroom reading center. The class chose a librarian to take charge, and an assistant to help. Mrs. English taught the students how to make cards for the books and how to keep the records.

Introducing A Book

When one of the children brought a book to class, he showed it to the other students. Then he told just enough about the story to make his friends want to read the book. One boy introduced a book in this way:

MODEL: A BOOK INTRODUCTION

This book, *The Bell of Atri,* is about a poor starving horse whose master did not feed him. The animal suffered so much that he had to ask the people in the town to help him. Can you guess what happened? You'll be surprised when you read this story for yourself.

CLASS ASSIGNMENT

A If you do not have a Book Corner, ask your teacher to let the class vote on one. Choose a librarian and an assistant librarian to take care of the books.

B Write the name of your favorite story on a card. Be sure to use capital letters to begin all important words in the title.

C Do you think each of the following is a good beginning sentence for a book introduction? Do you know the title to which each refers?
   1 In this story a great king learns a lesson from a spider.
   2 Would you like to be friends with two little Eskimo children who live in the frozen north?
   3 If you want to explore strange places, a hare will guide you to one.
   4 The boy in this story visited the Land of Giants.
   5 Do you know about the man who owned 500 hats?

D Introduce a book that you are lending to the classroom library.

THE LIBRARY

In addition to sharing books within our own classroom, there is another location where we can find even more books. This is the library. A library is a special place set aside to give us an opportunity to read and to learn. Here you will find hundreds of books that you may borrow for a period of time. Does your school have a library?

The library is a special place for all, not just for children. Adults visit it to borrow books or to find information. Because so many people use the library, there are certain rules like those on the next page that everyone should follow.

1   Behave quietly and courteously in the library. Because many people like to work in the library, it is necessary that everyone observes silence. We show kindness and thoughtfulness for others when we follow this regulation.

2   Treat books carefully, as if they were your own. Have clean hands when you handle books. Use a bookmark. Never turn down corners of the pages. Turn pages carefully and never mark a book.

3   Remember that the librarian is there to help you. When you are looking for a special book, you may need help in finding it. Never be too shy to ask for assistance. Tell the librarian the kind of book you are looking for, and he or she will locate it for you.

4   Leave extra books on a table. The librarian will return them to the proper place on the shelves.

Kinds of Books

There are hundreds of books in every library. They can be divided into two classes: *fiction* and *non-fiction*.

Fiction books are "make-believe" books. When we read books of fiction, we sometimes encounter elves, sail in magic balloons, or listen to talking animals. A fiction story is not true, but is written from the author's imagination.

Non-fiction books tell facts that are based on truth. We

may read about history, science, or people. These books help students with their schoolwork. For example, if you were studying about the Indians that lived in the West a long time ago, you might look for important facts about Indians. It would not be like a story made up about a little Indian boy or girl.

Of all the non-fiction books, there is one special group called *reference books*. These include dictionaries, encyclopedias, and atlases. Atlases are books of maps. Reference books are special, and are never taken from the library. If you need to use a reference book, the librarian will permit you to read it in the library.

Remembering Books

The children in Mrs. English's class did not wish to forget the books they read. They found that making a book record helped them remember each story. They answered these questions after reading a book:

What is the title of the book?
Who wrote the book?
What kind of book is it?
What character did I like best? Why?
What incident did I like best? Why?

When the children looked at their book records, they could remember the books they had read. Study the notes that one child made after she finished reading *Crow Boy*. This brief record was written on a card as follows:

BOOK RECORD

Name of Book	*Crow Boy*
Name of Author	Taro Yashima
Kind of Book	Fiction
Character I Liked Best	Chibi
An Incident I Enjoyed	The school teacher, Mr. Isobe, discovered Chibi's talent for imitating the sounds of crows. I liked this part of the story, because then all the children loved Chibi.

CLASS ASSIGNMENT

A   What are the five questions that should be answered in a book record?

B   Make a record of a book you have read. Be sure to include the five main parts.

Writing the Title of a Book

Mrs. English taught her students three rules to follow in writing titles of books. Be sure to learn these rules:

1   The first word in the title of a book always begins with a capital letter.

2   All important words in book titles begin with capital letters.

3   Words like *a, an, the, and, by, for, in,* and *of* are not capitalized unless each is the first word.

The following title is written correctly:

The Hundred Dresses

In a printed book, a different kind of type is used for titles of books. It is called *italics*. For example, Madeleine Brandeis wrote a book called *Little Indian Weaver*. If you were writing this title, you could not use italics. Instead, you would underline each word of the title.

Madeleine Brandeis wrote <u>Little Indian Weaver.</u>

CLASS ASSIGNMENT

Copy these titles. Use capital letters where they are needed.

moufflou	big brother
poppy seed cakes	letters from a cat
what katy did	the story of ferdinand
silver pennies	old mother west wind

A Game with Books

Mrs. English taught the class a game to play. One student would tell the class about a person he met in a book, but he did not tell the name of the character or the name of the book. The others had to guess who the person was. This is called *Guess My Name Game.*

MODEL: GUESS MY NAME GAME

On the way home from visiting a blind man I found a tiny hole in the dike. I knew that it would become larger and larger and the sea would soon flood our land. With my hand, I closed the hole. This kept the great sea from breaking the dike and flooding the country. Can you guess who I am?

Everyone knew the boy in this story was Peter of Haarlem, the young hero who saved his country from being destroyed by the sea.

Rules for Taking Care of Books

Mrs. English helped the class librarian and his assistant write some rules for taking care of the books in the Book Corner. These were the rules:

How to Take Care of Books

1   *Handle books gently.*
2   *Turn the pages carefully.*
3   *Use a book marker.*
4   *Place books where they belong.*
5   *Keep books from getting wet.*

CLASS ASSIGNMENT

A Guess the names of the characters in these stories:

    1 In an enchanted castle I slept for a hundred years. A brave knight rescued me through a wall of fire and I awakened. Later I married him. Who am I?

    2 There was not much to eat at our house, so my father and stepmother decided to take my brother and me to the forest. My brother filled his pockets with pebbles. These he scattered along the road and we were able to find our way back. What is my name?

    3 My fairy godmother dressed me in beautiful clothes and sent me to a ball in a pumpkin coach. I left the dance at twelve o'clock, in such a hurry that I lost one of my glass slippers. Who am I?

B Have everyone in your class think of some character in a book, then play the *Guess My Name Game.*

THE STORY TELLERS' CLUB

The children in Mrs. English's class had a story hour every Friday afternoon. During this period they talked about their favorite stories. Sometimes the teacher or one of the children told a story.

Mrs. English asked the students if they would like to have a story club. All in the room would be members of the club. They would meet once a week at the story-hour period. There were many things which they could do at their meetings. They could talk about stories; they could pantomime a story; they could pretend they were characters in a book and hold a conversation; they could dramatize a story; they could give a radio or television broadcast on a particular subject.

"Now you have a chance to vote as members of a club vote," said Mrs. English. "First, we must find out if our class wants to form a club. All who would like to have a story club, please stand." Mrs. English counted those who were standing. Then she asked, "Will all those who do not want a club, please stand." A few students rose this time. "Since more students want a club," said Mrs. English, "our class will organize a story club. Who can suggest a name for the club?"

Four students suggested names. The teacher wrote the names on the chalkboard. She then asked each one to write the name he liked best on a slip of paper. The name receiving the most votes was the Story Tellers' Club.

Mrs. English said, "It is time now to close our meeting. The Story Tellers' Club will meet again next Friday at two o'clock. Jerome will be chairman of the meeting. Ruth, Bill, Martin, and Wendy will help him. These students will meet with me after school. We will arrange an interesting program for our next meeting."

A Club Meeting

When the day for the meeting came, Jerome acted as chairman. He called the meeting to order, and stated that the five students in charge of the meeting were going to dramatize the story of "The Country Mouse and the City Mouse."

In the play, Martin took the part of the Country Mouse, while Bill was the City Mouse. Ruth was a woman in the city, and Wendy was a maid. They forgot for the moment that they were children in school, and put themselves in place of the mouse that lived in the country and the mouse that lived in the city.

A MEETING OF THE STORY TELLERS' CLUB

JEROME: The meeting will please come to order. For our program this week, we shall present the story of "The Country Mouse and the City Mouse." Imagine you are in the home of Mr. Country Mouse. Mr. City Mouse is his guest. It is evening. (Martin and Bill enter the room.)

COUNTRY MOUSE: Well, well, my friend, welcome to my house. Sit down and let us dine.

CITY MOUSE (sniffing): Thank you, friend. (He looks around.) You like it here in the country?

COUNTRY MOUSE: Indeed I do, sir! I would not live in any other place. Do have some of this sweet corn.

CITY MOUSE (nibbling at the corn): Why, you live an ant's life out here away from everything.

COUNTRY MOUSE: Try some of these fresh wheat grains, they're delicious.

CITY MOUSE (smiling at the food): Why, this is poor fare. I have much better food at my home. Come back to town and enjoy a delicious meal with me!

COUNTRY MOUSE: When? Tonight? It is already too late!

CITY MOUSE: We shall be there in a jiffy. Come, my friend. (Mr. Country Mouse looks around his simple home and sighs. He packs his bag and accompanies his city friend.)

JEROME: We will pause a few moments while our friends travel to the city. It is now midnight. They have arrived at the apartment of Mr. City Mouse.

CITY MOUSE: Now, sir, I shall be the host. Let me take your bag and your walking stick. (He places them in a corner.) Let us dine before going to bed.

COUNTRY MOUSE (gazing at the food heaped on the table): My, my, you are very *rich.*

CITY MOUSE: Look! Here are honey, fruit, and sharp cheese.

COUNTRY MOUSE: They make my mouth water.

CITY MOUSE (with his eye on the door):   Let us eat, drink, and be merry, my friend.

COUNTRY MOUSE: What a fine home you have, City Mouse! How very well off you are!

CITY MOUSE: I am quite rich, my friend, but wait. You will see more by and by. (Suddenly a women enters the room. The two frightened mice scamper into a corner.)

CITY MOUSE (creeping out as soon as it is safe):   Awful, was it not?

COUNTRY MOUSE: Indeed, my friend, that was a *very* narrow escape.

CITY MOUSE (with a city man's indifference):   Let's forget all about it, Country Mouse, and eat. Here are some juicy figs. (As they begin to eat, a maid enters to get a pot of honey and some cheese. Her skirts brush the frightened mice as she passes.)

COUNTRY MOUSE (in a whisper):   Squeak! Squeak! Let us hide.

CITY MOUSE (also in a whisper): Yes sir! (They both run into the corner. They come out again when the maid has gone.)

COUNTRY MOUSE: Well, sir, I won't eat any more in town. You may do as you like, but—

CITY MOUSE (trying to be brave): Don't tell me you are leaving!

COUNTRY MOUSE: I am, friend. You eat what you want, but always in fear of your life.

CITY MOUSE (laughing): Nonsense, Country Mouse! Why, it's all in the game.

COUNTRY MOUSE: Don't tell me that, City Mouse. I'm going back to the country and eat my corn and wheat afraid of no one. No more of your city life for me! (The City Mouse hands Mr. Country Mouse his bag and walking stick, and walks him to the door.)

COUNTRY MOUSE: Thank you for the visit and the food, City Mouse. Good Night!

JEROME: So our little story ends. Thank you for your attention. I hope you enjoyed our skit.

CLASS ASSIGNMENT

A Have a vote in your class to see how many students wish to form a story club.

B Select a name for your club.

C Choose students to give the same program as the Story Tellers' Club gave.

D Plan a program for another club meeting. Let several students pantomime a story as another student tells it.

The Young Detective Game

At some meetings, the Story Tellers' Club played the *Young Detective Game*. Mrs. English appointed one student to tell a story, then selected twelve others to act as detectives. The detectives listened very carefully. The judge asked them questions quickly, one after another, about the story. Mrs. English was the judge for the game.

It was Louise Young's turn to tell a story. She prepared it the night before by reading the fable "The Hare and the Tortoise." The next day at the story hour she told it like this:

THE HARE AND THE TORTOISE

One day a hare met a tortoise. He began to ridicule her short, clumsy feet and her slow pace. "I am as swift as the wind," boasted the Hare. "Don't you wish that your legs were long and slender like mine?"

"I know you are as swift as the wind," answered the Tortoise, "but I think I can beat you in a race."

The Hare laughed loudly at this reply but agreed to the race. They asked Mr. Fox to map out the course and to fix the goal.

When the day for the race finally came, the Hare and the Tortoise stood together on the starting line. "One, two, three, go!" shouted the Fox. They were off!

In a short while, the Hare was far ahead of the Tortoise. He was hungry, and so he stopped to eat. He felt a little tired after his lunch, so he lay down by the road and fell fast asleep.

The Tortoise plodded steadily ahead with a slow and even pace. She never stopped, not even for a moment.

Suddenly the Hare awoke. The Tortoise was nowhere to be seen. He bounded toward the goal line as fast as he could. The Tortoise had already arrived!

"Ah," said the Fox, "the Tortoise wins the race. A slow but steady pace is swifter in the long run than sudden leaps and bounds."

When Louise finished the story, Mrs. English asked the "detectives" questions. Good detectives see everything that is done, and hear everything that is said. Some of the children did not prove to be very good sleuths. These are questions the judge asked:

JUDGE: What animals agreed to race?
GEORGE: The Hare and the Tortoise.
JUDGE: Who told the Hare and the Tortoise where to begin and how far to run?
BRUNO: Was it a dog, Mrs. English?
JUDGE: No, it wasn't a dog. Can you tell us, Stephen?
STEPHEN: The Fox mapped out the course and fixed the goal.

JUDGE: What else did the Fox do?

ELEANOR: The Fox counted "One, two, three" and told them when to go.

JUDGE: Did the Hare run faster than the Tortoise?

VERONICA: Yes, Mrs. English, the Hare ran very fast.

JUDGE: Carol, how did the Tortoise move?

CAROL: The Tortoise moved very slowly, but she moved very steadily, too.

JUDGE: Why do you think the Hare stopped to eat while he was racing?

ANNA: He ran so fast that he was quite sure he could overtake the Tortoise.

JUDGE: Did the Tortoise pass where the Hare was sleeping?

EDWARD: Yes, but the Hare was fast asleep and didn't even see the Tortoise pass.

JUDGE: Did the Hare win the race?

SAMUEL: No, the Tortoise won the race.

JUDGE: Why didn't the Hare win?

CLARA: He stopped to eat, and then fell asleep.

JUDGE: What lesson do you learn from the story?

JANET: The Hare runs faster than the Tortoise.

JUDGE: No, that isn't the *lesson*. The Fox told us what the lesson is.

ANDREW: The Fox said, "A slow but steady pace is swifter in the long run than sudden leaps and bounds."

CLASS ASSIGNMENT

Play the *Young Detective Game* in your classroom. Your teacher will appoint a storyteller and twelve detectives. Any of the following stories may be used, or one that the class has read.

1	Ferdinand the Bull	4	How the Camel Got His Hump
2	The Golden Goose	5	Pandora's Box
3	Dick Whittington and His Cat	6	The Ugly Duckling

THE VAST WORLD

The wonderful world in which we live is quite large. The United States is only one of the nations of the world, but it takes several days to travel from one seacoast to the other by train. If one country is so large, how vast the entire world must be!

Today it takes much less time to travel from place to place than it did in the days of Columbus and the early explorers. It used to take sailing ships months to make a journey that steamships can now make in a few days. Airplanes travel even faster than steamships. People in the countries of Europe and Asia now seem closer to America because the means of traveling are so much better.

Inventions that make distances seem smaller are the radio and television. Frequently, we hear broadcasts from Europe, Asia, or South America.

Broadcasting

Mrs. English's class had studied about the different means of travel. They decided to give three radio broadcasts. One would be on transportation by water, a second on transportation by land, and a third on transportation by air. In each broadcast they planned to show the difference between travel in the past and travel today.

Here is the broadcast on transportation by water:

MODEL: A RADIO OR TELEVISION BROADCAST

ANNOUNCER: Good afternoon, boys and girls. This broadcast will tell you about transportation by water, yesterday and today. Our first speaker, Steve Parker, will tell how the people traveled by water long ago.

STEVE: The first boats were merely floating logs. The early people sat on these crude boats and paddled themselves across the stream with their hands. Soon they discovered that the logs moved faster if they used paddles made of wood instead of using their hands.

ANNOUNCER: Thank you, Steve. We enjoyed your talk. Frank Cary will now tell us about the first *real* boat.

FRANK: Soon people learned to hollow out logs to use for boats. These were known as dugouts. The dugout was the beginning of what we call a canoe today.

ANNOUNCER: Thank you, Frank, for telling us about the dugout. Our next speaker is Juanita Perez.

JUANITA: People soon learned to fasten pieces of wood together and shape them into a boat. These took the place of dugouts and canoes. They also used oars instead of paddles. These boats became known as rowboats.

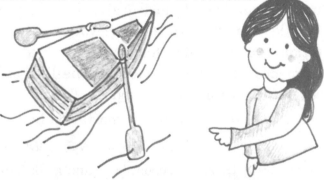

ANNOUNCER: Thank you for telling us about the rowboat, Juanita. Edward Olson will now tell us something about the sailboat.

EDWARD: As time went on, people noticed that the wind helped them to paddle or row their boats. They decided to let the wind move the vessel. A pole, called a mast, was placed in the boat. Sails, made of cloth, were attached to the mast. This is how the sailboat originated!

ANNOUNCER: That was very interesting, Ed. We will now ask Tom Latz to tell us about the steamboat.

TOM: After the invention of the steam engine, people began to dream about using this power to move boats. In 1807, Robert Fulton launched the first steamboat, which he called the *Clermont*. At last the day had come when people no longer depended on the wind to move boats.

ANNOUNCER: Thank you, Tom. Fulton must have been a very happy man when he saw the *Clermont* moving without sails, paddles, or oars. Our last speaker is Betty Owens, who will tell us about a ship undreamed of in earlier days.

BETTY: Many improvements have been made since the days of the first steamships. Ships that cross the ocean today are as big as city blocks. Some of the passenger ships have swimming pools, tennis courts, libraries, and ballrooms. These are called ocean liners.

ANNOUNCER: Thank you, Betty. I'm sure our radio audience has enjoyed hearing this program about transportation by water, yesterday and today. Next week, at the same time, we shall present the second in our series of broadcasts, "Travel by Land." We hope you will be listening. Good-bye and thank you. This is your announcer, Helen Wilson.

CLASS ASSIGNMENT

A   Present the model broadcast in your classroom.

B   Prepare a broadcast on any one of the following topics:

1   Transportation by land
2   Transportation by air
3   Story of cotton
4   Life among the early North American Indians
5   American heroines
6   A farmer's work in spring

Riddles

The class learned much about means of traveling when they prepared their radio broadcasts. One day, Mrs. English suggested they make up riddles about boats, trains, automobiles, airplanes, and other ways people travel. The riddle was to describe the vehicle, without mentioning its name. The class would guess what means of travel the riddle described.

MODEL: A RIDDLE

I travel on steel rails under the city. Rushing through dark tunnels, I carry passengers swiftly to their destinations. Can you guess what I am?

Note that the words *subway train* are not in the riddle, but all the children knew the answer was a subway train.

CLASS ASSIGNMENT

A   Guess the answers to the following riddles:
1   I am long and slender. One paddle moves me lightly and easily through the water. The Indians traveled in me. Today people use me on rivers and lakes for sport. What am I?

2 I have a narrow metal body, two large rear wheels, and one small front wheel. The person driving me sits up very high. I am used primarily by farmers. What is my name?

3 I am the fastest means of transportation. I have bright silver wings. Like a bird, I fly through the sky. Can you name me?

B Tell a riddle about one of the following vehicles:

An automobile	A bicycle	A sailboat
A snowmobile	An ocean liner	A truck
An airplane	A rocket	A bus
A freight train	A motorcycle	A sled

C Tell a riddle about an animal that you have seen in a zoo.

CHORAL SPEAKING

Let us again prepare for choral speaking by doing some tuning-up exercises.

TUNING-UP EXERCISES

Breathing:

Inhale slowly as if smelling a flower. Feel your ribs expand and your lungs fill with fresh air. Hold the breath for ten counts. Exhale slowly with the sound of *puff, puff, puff.*

Enunciation:

A pleasing voice has *resonance:* that is, a full musical quality. Humming will help you to gain this round tone. Close your lips lightly and hum. Hold the sound for ten counts. If you do this correctly, your lips will tickle. Repeat several times. Say the following line, holding the sounds of *ng:*

The bell sang its song of "Bing, bang, bong."

Pronounce the following words, holding the sounds of *m, n,* and *ng:*

moon	many	throng	come
moan	plum	mountain	long
song	young	none	rumble

Now our voices should sound like one voice when we say a poem together. Practice by reciting "Hey, Bug!"

HEY, BUG!
by Lilian Moore

Hey, bug, stay!
Don't run away.
I know a game that we can play.

I'll hold my fingers very still
and you can climb a finger-hill.

No, no.
Don't go.

Here's a wall—a tower, too,
A tiny bug town, just for you.
I've a cookie. You have some.
Take this oatmeal cookie crumb.

Hey, bug, stay!
Hey, bug!
Hey!

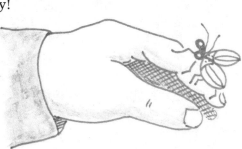

"The Duel"

Listen as this next poem, "The Duel," is read. Try to feel the rhythm or beat in the poem. Listen for the rhyming words at the end of some lines. If there is any word or part of the poem that you do not understand, use your dictionary or ask your teacher about it.

After you have listened to the poem and feel you understand it, you may recite "The Duel" together. The girls will say the first verse, the boys, the second verse; then boys and girls together will take the third and fourth verses. One student, or a small group of students, may say the solo parts.

THE DUEL

by Eugene Field

Girls:
The gingham dog and the calico cat
Side by side on the table sat;
'Twas half-past twelve, and (what do you think!),
Nor one nor t'other had slept a wink!
  The old Dutch clock and the Chinese plate
  Appeared to know as sure as fate
There was going to be a terrible spat.

Solo:
(I wasn't there; I simply state
What was told to me by the Chinese plate!)

Boys:
The gingham dog went, "Bow-wow-wow!"
And the calico cat replied, "Mee-ow!"
The air was littered, an hour or so,
With bits of gingham and calico,
  While the old Dutch clock in the chimney-place
  Up with its hands before its face,
For it always dreaded a family row!

Solo:

(Now mind: I'm only telling you
What the old Dutch clock declares is true!)

All:

The Chinese plate looked very blue,
And wailed, "Oh, dear! what shall we do!"
But the gingham dog and the calico cat
Wallowed this way and tumbled that,
    Employing every tooth and claw
    In the awfullest way you ever saw—
And, oh! how the gingham and calico flew!

Solo:

(Don't fancy I exaggerate—
I got my news from the Chinese plate!)

All:

Next morning, where the two had sat
They found no trace of dog or cat;
And some folks think unto this day
That burglars stole that pair away!
    But the truth about the cat and pup
    Is this: they ate each other up!
Now what do you really think of that!

Solo:

(The old Dutch clock it told me so,
And that is how I came to know.)

PART TWO

GRAMMAR

CHAPTER ONE

Sentences

A sentence is a group of words expressing a complete thought.

Not every group of words makes a sentence. Here are two groups of words:

> Fish swim.
> At two o'clock on Saturday afternoon

The first group has only two words, but it is a sentence because it tells that fish swim. In the second group there are six words. This is not a sentence because it does not express a complete thought.

Now look at the words in these two columns. The words in Column One are not sentences. The words in Column Two are sentences. Copy the sentences in Column Two and put a period at the end of each sentence.

COLUMN ONE	COLUMN TWO
Brings our mail	The postman brings our mail
Ruth and Helen	Ruth and Helen attend our school
The safety rules	I know the safety rules for bike riding

COLUMN ONE	COLUMN TWO
In Virginia	My grandparents live in Virginia
White rabbits	I have seen many white rabbits
Worked hard all day	The men worked hard all day
With her dog	Becky often plays with her dog
Vacation in the mountains	We enjoyed our vacation in the mountains
Our country is	Our country is the United States of America
The mayor	The mayor came to our school today

DECLARATIVE SENTENCES

A sentence which states a fact is called a *declarative sentence*. A sentence must express a complete thought. Study these words:

Sang a song

This is not a complete thought because it does not tell who or what sang a song. We can make a declarative sentence by adding a word to complete the thought:

Maria sang a song.

This is a declarative sentence because it states a fact about Maria. Notice the mark of punctuation at the end of the sentence. It is called a *period*. The main work of a period is to say "Stop! This is the end of a sentence." It is always used after a declarative sentence. Learn these rules:

> **A declarative sentence states a fact.**
> **A declarative sentence is followed by a period.**
> **The first word of a declarative sentence begins with a capital letter.**

EXERCISE 1

Copy these declarative sentences. Place a period at the end of each.

1 My sister has big fuzzy slippers
2 I like corn on the cob
3 David toasted marshmallows at camp
4 Ellen is an interesting girl
5 We should eat fresh fruit every day
6 The president lives in Washington, D.C.
7 Our school is a large building
8 There are sixteen ounces in one pound
9 The children love their grandmother
10 We watched the hockey game
11 Jim goes to bed at eight o'clock
12 Susan is in the third grade
13 My cousins live far away
14 Children like to play outdoors
15 Judy went to a party
16 I have three brothers

146

EXERCISE 2

Copy the following sentences. Begin the first word of each sentence with a capital letter, and put a period at the end of each sentence.

1   milk is a perfect food
2   a stitch in time saves nine
3   the children skated on the frozen pond
4   woolen clothing is warm
5   oranges grow on trees
6   good books are good friends
7   we brush our teeth twice a day
8   my brother and I sleep in a bunk bed
9   some paper is made of rags
10 the leaves of the trees have changed their colors

EXERCISE 3

Some of the following groups of words are sentences and some are not. Copy each group of words. Put a period at the end of each group of words that expresses a complete thought, and write NS (for "not a sentence") at the end of each group if the words do not express a complete thought.

1   Caterpillars change into butterflies
2   Soft feathers
3   Baby chicks have soft feathers
4   The robin's breast is red
5   On the side of a hill
6   Cotton is soft and fluffy
7   We saw a giraffe at the zoo
8   Buttercups were in bloom on the side of the hill
9   Elephants in the zoo
10 A dozen peaches
11 A duckling is a little duck
12 My dog has a short tail

INTERROGATIVE SENTENCES

We know that a sentence is a group of words expressing a complete thought. We have learned that a sentence which states a fact is called a declarative sentence. A period is placed at the end of a declarative sentence.

Another kind of sentence is used to ask questions. This is called an *interrogative sentence*. We place a *question mark* at the end of every interrogative sentence. Interrogative sentences begin with such words as *When, Where, Who, Why, How, Is, Are, Will, Do,* and *Did.*

1 When is Flag Day?
2 Where is the telephone?
3 Will you play with me?
4 Did you win the game?
5 Are you going to the library?
6 Is this your skateboard?
7 Why are you late?
8 Do you study your lessons?
9 How do you feel?
10 Who is your brother?

Notice the question mark at the end of these sentences. Learn these rules:

An interrogative sentence asks a question.

An interrogative sentence is followed by a question mark.

An interrogative sentence begins with a capital letter.

Here is a jingle to help you remember the end punctuation of an asking sentence:

I'm a little question mark;
To you this rule I send:
When writing an asking sentence,
Please put me at the end.

EXERCISE 4

Copy these sentences. Place a question mark after each interrogative sentence and a period after each declarative sentence.

1 How many seasons are there
2 There are four seasons
3 Where was Liz born
4 Liz was born in Chicago
5 Did you use a period after each declarative sentence
6 We always use a period after a sentence which states a fact
7 How many stars are there in our flag
8 Who has had the measles
9 Some dwarfs live in caves
10 Is your father at home
11 Are those your goldfish
12 The team played their last game
13 Do you like to study history
14 He forgot to buy a pencil
15 Pandora was a curious person
16 Mr. Lopez is our coach
17 Why did you call him
18 The twins wore the same colors
19 What are tadpoles
20 The sun gives heat

EXCLAMATORY SENTENCES

We have already studied two kinds of sentences. We learned that a declarative sentence states a fact, and that an interrogative sentence asks a question.

Another kind of sentence expresses strong feeling or surprise. We call this an *exclamatory sentence*.

These are exclamatory sentences. They express strong or

sudden emotions:

> What a scare he gave us!
> What a beautiful picture that is!
> How I miss my brother!

We place an *exclamation point* at the end of an exclamatory sentence. Learn these rules:

An exclamatory sentence expresses a strong or sudden emotion.

An exclamatory sentence is followed by an exclamation point.

An exclamatory sentence begins with a capital letter.

EXERCISE 5

Copy these exclamatory sentences. Put an exclamation point at the end.

1 What a delightful time we had at the party
2 How well Jean plays the violin
3 What fun we had at the circus
4 How happy I am to see you
5 How you startled me
6 What a wonderful story that is
7 How the wind blows
8 How quickly you returned
9 How cold it is in this room
10 What a beautiful rainbow I saw
11 How bravely the soldiers fought
12 How frightened I was

IMPERATIVE SENTENCES

Some sentences give a command or make a request. These are called *imperative sentences*. An imperative sentence may have the subject *you* understood.

These are imperative sentences:

Tippy, jump for the bone.
(You) Be polite to others.
John, please open the window.

Learn these rules:

An imperative sentence gives a command or makes a request.

An imperative sentence is usually followed by a period.

An imperative sentence begins with a capital letter.

EXERCISE 6

Copy each of these imperative sentences. Place a period at the end.

1 Stand still, Larry
2 Sing that beautiful song
3 Always stop, look, and listen before you cross the street
4 Be quiet

5   Please cut the grass on Saturday
6   David, please help your brother with the work
7   Open the door
8   Nancy, read the first paragraph
9   Children, please clean the lunchroom
10   Patrick, please mail this package

MORE SENTENCES

We have now studied four kinds of sentences—a *declarative sentence,* an *interrogative sentence,* an *exclamatory sentence,* and an *imperative sentence.* Declarative sentences and imperative sentences are followed by *periods.* Interrogative sentences are followed by *question marks.* Exclamatory sentences are followed by *exclamation points.*

Tennis is my favorite sport.   (A declarative sentence)

Do you know all the rules?   (An interrogative sentence)

What good fudge this is!   (An exclamatory sentence)

Do not tear the newspaper.   (An imperative sentence)

The first word of every sentence begins with a capital letter.

Now we will review or summarize the *end punctuation* of sentences. The class will be divided into three groups. The groups may introduce themselves in the following manner:

First Group: We're the willing periods.
We're always in demand,
When a person states a fact
And issues a command.

Second Group: We're the curious question marks.
When a question you must ask,
We'll end the sentence for you;
It's such an easy task.

Third Group: We're the exclamation points.
A surprise we indicate;
For strong or sudden emotion
Use us, please; don't wait!

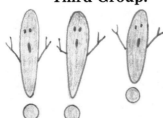

Three students will rise together (one from each group). In turn, each will name the type of sentence called for by the end punctuation he or she represents.

EXERCISE 7

Copy these sentences. Place the correct punctuation mark at the end.

1 What is the name of that television program
2 Don't step in that wet cement
3 Eat some vegetables every day
4 Will you teach me to play that game
5 Tell me when the taxicab comes
6 The contest was held last Friday
7 How happy I am today
8 Tell me a story about knights and dragons
9 That boy has five sisters
10 What have you made
11 Say the words clearly and distinctly
12 I know how to use the dictionary

EXERCISE 8

Copy these sentences. Put *D* after each declarative sentence; *I* after each interrogative sentence; *E* after each exclamatory sentence; and *IMP* after each imperative sentence.

1 Coal is mined in Pennsylvania.
2 Where do citrus fruits grow?
3 How beautiful the sunset is!
4 Write the words on the line.
5 Can you play hockey?
6 Last summer we went to Yellowstone National Park.
7 What ocean is east of the United States?
8 The United States imports coffee.
9 Do your work neatly.
10 In what country is Rome?
11 What is a fable?
12 What a delicious meal this is!

SUBJECT AND PREDICATE

A sentence contains two parts: the *subject* and the *predicate*.

The most important word in the sentence is the *verb*. The verb, or *predicate,* tells something about the subject. There cannot be a sentence without a verb. The predicate, or verb, in the following sentences is in italics:

> The ship *docked* yesterday.
> Canadians often *see* the northern lights.
> The sun *gives* energy.

Read each sentence again, omitting the verb. You will see that the sentence has no meaning without the predicate.

The *subject* of the sentence is that part which names the *person, place, or thing about which something is said.* In the following sentences the subject is in italics:

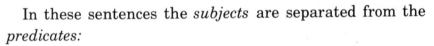

Mother takes photographs.
Our *team* won the game.
A *pigeon* waddled across the path.

In these sentences the *subjects* are separated from the *predicates:*

>   S   P
> A *telescope*/*magnifies* an object.
>   S   P
> The *birds*/*flew* to their nests.
> S   P
> *I*/*like* chocolate ice cream.

Finding the Predicate

The predicate, or verb, in a sentence tells what a person or a thing *does* or *did*. To find the predicate of a sentence, ask *what the subject did* or *does:*

> Carol wrote a book report.
>
> What did Carol *do?*
> Carol wrote.
> *Wrote* is the *predicate* of the sentence.
>
> The wind howled through the trees.
> What did the wind *do?*
> The wind howled.
> *Howled* is the predicate of the sentence.

A word that tells what the subject *does* or *did* is called a *verb*. It is the *predicate* of the sentence.

Finding the Subject

The word that names the person, place, or thing talked about is a *noun* or a *pronoun*. It is the *subject* of the sentence. A noun may be either a proper noun or a common noun.

To find the subject of a sentence, ask *"who?"* or *"what?"* before the verb.

> The wind howled through the trees.
> *What* howled?
> The wind howled.
> *Wind* is a common noun, and the subject of the sentence. A common noun names *any one* of a group of persons, places or things.

Carol wrote a book report.

Who wrote?

Carol wrote.

Carol is a proper noun, and the subject of the sentence. A proper noun names a *special* person, place or thing. It begins with a capital letter.

EXERCISE 9

Read the following sentences carefully. Ask yourself the two questions under each sentence. Write the *subject* and the *predicate* of each sentence. The first one is done for you.

1   The bluebirds flew away.
    What flew?   *bluebirds* (subject)
    Bluebirds did what?   *flew* (predicate)

2   The rabbit hopped across the lawn.
    What hopped?
    Rabbit did what?

3   The boys sing.
    Who sing?
    Boys do what?

4   Flowers grow.
    What grow?
    Flowers do what?

5   Snow covered the ground.
    What covered?
    Snow did what?

6   The boat rocked gently.
    What rocked?
    The boat did what?

7   The children like summer.
    Who like?
    Children do what?

8   Blossoms covered the tree.
    What covered?
    Blossoms did what?

9   Brad washed Dad's car.
    Who washed?
    Brad did what?

10   Valerie wrote a poem.
    Who wrote?
    Valerie did what?

EXERCISE 10

Copy the following sentences. Draw one line under the subject and two lines under the predicate. Find the predicate first, and then ask the question "who?" or "what?" before the predicate to find the subject. The first sentence is done for you.

1 The <u>band</u> <u>marched</u> in the parade.
2 I enjoyed this movie.
3 The children went for bicycle rides.
4 Pedro went to the library.
5 The carpenter fixed the screen door.
6 The beaver has a wide tail.
7 We saw beautiful fireworks.
8 Janet ran to the park.
9 Peanuts grow in Georgia.
10 The horse galloped down the road.

EXERCISE 11

Copy the following sentences. Draw two lines under the predicate and one line under the subject. Draw a vertical line to separate the subject from the predicate.

EXAMPLE: *SUBJECT*   *PREDICATE*

The <u>birds</u> / <u>twitter</u>.

1 John skates.
2 Bees buzz.
3 Coffee perks.
4 My father laughs.
5 Baby sleeps.

6 The ocean roars.
7 Rain splashes.
8 Corn pops.
9 Fire crackles.
10 Jenny sings.

WORD STUDY

Dictionary Skills

A trip through Wordland would be confusing, if it were not for that wonderful wizard of words—the dictionary. First, let us take a walk down Alphabet Lane. All the words in the dictionary are in alphabetical order. You'll want to know the alphabet before using this important book of words.

EXERCISE 12

Repeat the letters of the alphabet in the proper order.

EXERCISE 13

Copy the following letters. Write the letter that comes before and after each letter.

b	n	f
s	o	e
x	c	u
m	r	j

EXERCISE 14

Rewrite the scrambled letters in *alphabetical* order. You should make a word from each group.

EXAMPLE: wco—cow

tosc	enbt	pmo	rof
somt	yocp	mfil	gesg
ristf	micph	yocphp	rolfo
edep	nay	tac	ojy
ria	stol	wlfo	icyt

Synonyms

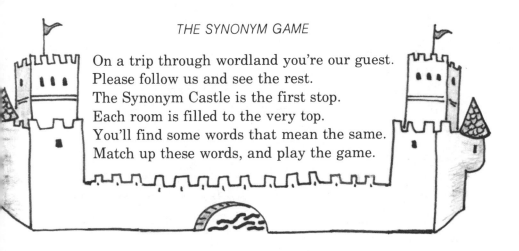

THE SYNONYM GAME

On a trip through wordland you're our guest.
Please follow us and see the rest.
The Synonym Castle is the first stop.
Each room is filled to the very top.
You'll find some words that mean the same.
Match up these words, and play the game.

Here are pairs of words that are *synonyms*. They mean nearly the same:

small—little	town—city
shiny—bright	rip—tear

EXERCISE 15

Copy the following rhymes. Fill in the blanks with correct synonyms for the words in italics.

1 The bus through the *city* goes up and down,
  It moves along quickly to the next_____ .

2 A *tear* in your paper you don't want to see.
  If you're not careful, a_____there will be.

3 The *shiny* stars fill the dark sky at night.
  They color the world; they look so _____ .

4 My new baby brother is very *small*.
  His_____fingers can't hold a ball.

EXERCISE 16

Copy the following sentences. Write a synonym in place of the word in italics.

1   Our *town* has many people.
2   Our new car has *shiny* bumpers.
3   The *tear* in the curtain could not be seen.
4   The *small* boy ran to the swings.

Antonyms

In Wordland you'll discover words called *antonyms*. These are words of opposite meaning. Let's read a rhyme to help us learn antonyms.

> If I'm *out*, I can't be *in*.
> If it's *thick*, it can't be *thin*.
> If it's *good*, it can't be *bad*.
> If I'm *happy*, I can't be *sad*.

Can you find the antonyms in the rhyme? In this lesson let us take a special look at the antonyms *thick* and *thin*. Notice how these words are used in the following sentences:

My shoes have *thick* soles.
My mother's slippers have *thin* soles.

Thick means much space between one side and the opposite side; *thin* means little space between one side and the opposite side.

EXERCISE 17

Copy the following sentences. Write the antonym for the word printed in italics.

1   This is a *thin* slice of bread.
2   Some meats are cut *thick*.
3   This gravy is very *thick*.
4   The bag was made from *thin* strips of leather.
5   My hair is very *thick*.
6   The knife has a *thin* blade.
7   The sign was printed on a *thin* piece of cardboard.
8   The pond was covered with *thick* ice.
9   I need a *thin* piece of wire.
10 This glass is very *thick*.
11 This is a *thick* book.
12 Please give me a *thin* piece of cake.

Homonyms

A tour through Wordland would not be complete without a visit to the House of Homonyms. Here you'll find words that sound alike, but are not spelled alike, and do not mean the same thing. These words are called *homonyms*.

"KNOW" and "NO"

Know means to have a knowledge of or to be familiar with. *No* means none or not any. The words *know* and *no* are called *homonyms*.

Read this sentence:

Did you *know* there are *no* pink elephants in the zoo?

Learn to use *know* and *no* correctly in the sentences you write.

EXERCISE 18

Copy the following sentences. Use the word *no* or *know* correctly in each sentence.

1   I have_____time to waste.
2   Do you_____the correct answer?
3   I _____you can do this work easily.
4   We have had_____snow this winter.
5   Do you_____the capital of Pennsylvania?
6   You_____these apples are not ripe.
7   I do not_____how to make a pie.
8   We have_____place to put the poster.
9   Martin does not_____who called.
10 Ricardo wanted to_____your address.
11 There are_____crayons in the box.
12 Have you_____paper?
13 I do not_____your name.
14 There are_____penguins here.
15 Do you _____that teacher?
16 We_____that cows give milk.
17 That dog has _____tail.
18 My parents_____Mr. King.

"SEE" and "SEA"

Did you ever go down to *sea?*
Tell me, please, what did you *see?*
Waves so high, they reached the sky?
Or maybe just the wind passing by?

This rhyme contains two homonyms. The words *see* and *sea* sound alike, but they are not spelled alike, and they do not have the same meaning. The word *sea* means an ocean. The word *see* means to look at with the eyes.

EXERCISE 19

Copy the following sentences. Write the word *sea* or *see* in each blank.

1 Look closely and you will_____the ladybug.
2 Did you_____the sun rise this morning?
3 The waves rose high on the stormy_____ .
4 Can you_____the house from the plane window?
5 Columbus liked to watch the_____ .
6 We cannot_____air.
7 The blind man cannot_____ .
8 I_____the ship in the distance.
9 Life at_____can be dangerous.
10 Sailors love the_____ .
11 At night we_____the moon.
12 The moon was shining on the calm_____ .

"BUY" and "BY"

Buy and *by* are also homonyms you'll meet in Wordland. Learn to tell them apart. Remember homonyms are words that sound alike, but are not spelled alike, and do not mean the same thing. *Buy* means to purchase something. *By* means near, or at the side of.

> I will *buy* a chocolate bar.
> Mary sat *by* me in the car.

EXERCISE 20

Copy the following sentences. Choose the correct word, *by* or *buy*, in each sentence.

1   Did you (by, buy) a blue hat?
2   The old woman sat (by, buy) the window.
3   She saw the wild geese fly (by, buy).
4   The children will (by, buy) a present for their mother.
5   (By, buy) the house stood a tall tree.
6   When did you (by, buy) that umbrella?
7   Grandfather sits in the chair (by, buy) the TV.
8   Will you (by, buy) some flowers?
9   The parade passed (by, buy) our house.
10 Did your father (by, buy) a new car?

Contractions

"I'M"

On our way to school, or to somewhere else, we sometimes take a short cut. We can take short cuts in our speaking and writing, too. When introduced to someone for the first time, we may say, "I'm glad to meet you." The word *I'm* is a contraction of the two words, *I am*. We say or write *one word* instead of *two words*. In place of the *a* in *am*, a little mark called an *apostrophe* is used. The apostrophe takes the place of a letter or letters that have been left out when two words are written as one. The word *I'm* has three parts—the capital letter *I*, the apostrophe, and the letter *m*. *I'm* is called a *contraction*.

WORDS	CONTRACTION	CHANGES
I am	I'm	Take out the *a*. Put in the apostrophe (').

EXERCISE 21

Use the contraction *I'm* in place of the words *I am* in each of
the following sentences:

1   I am going home.
2   I am very tired.
3   I am helping my mother.
4   I am not very busy.
5   Now I am ready to work.
6   I am going to save stamps for a hobby.
7   I am in a play at school.
8   I am nine years old.
9   After dinner I am going to play the piano.
10   I am reading an exciting book.

EXERCISE 22

For practice in saying *I'm,* play the "Where are you?" game.
Each boy and girl pretends that he or she is somewhere, such
as in the library, at home, or at a baseball game. The
teacher, or a student, asks, "Where are you, James?" James
answers by saying, "I'm in the library" or "I'm at home." If
any child says "I am" instead of "I'm," that person is out of
the game.

"CAN'T"

We often use a contraction in speaking and writing the words *can* and *not*. The new word is *can't*. The word *can* means *is able,* but the contraction, *can't,* means *is not able.*

We *can't* go to the game.

WORDS	CONTRACTION	CHANGES
can not	can't	Take out the *n* and *o*. Put in the apostrophe (').

EXERCISE 23

Copy the following sentences. Use the contraction for the words *can not* in each sentence.

1 Carlos said, "I can not find my sneakers."
2 Ships can not travel in shallow water.
3 If I can not do it at first, I will try again.
4 Alex can not swim very well.
5 Drivers can not see far in a fog.
6 We can not find the keys to the car.
7 Pineapples can not grow in a cold climate.
8 We can not live without air.
9 He can not beat his sister in a race.
10 A turtle can not move very fast.
11 They can not play the game because of the rain.
12 My little brother can not tell time.

EXERCISE 24   [Chapter Challenge]

Read this paragraph carefully, and then answer orally the questions that follow:

A DAY AT THE OLYMPICS

¹Finally the day for the Clearfield Olympics had come. ²Who would be this year's champ? ³Luis stood in line with the other nine-year-old skateboard winners from the city playgrounds. ⁴"I'm going to give it my all!" thought Luis, as he heard the starting whistle blow. ⁵Down the hill raced the skateboards on their thick, shiny wheels. ⁶The first person to cross the finish line was Luis! ⁷He could see the happy faces of his team as he walked toward the judges to receive his prize.

1　Do all the sentences express complete thoughts?
2　What do you call the mark at the end of the sixth sentence?
3　What kind of sentence is the second sentence?
4　What kind of mark follows an imperative or commanding sentence?
5　What kind of sentence is the third sentence?
6　Name a contraction in the fourth sentence.
7　Name an antonym for the word *thick* in the fifth sentence.
8　What kind of sentence is the first sentence?
9　Spell the homonym for the word *see* in the seventh sentence.
10　Name a synonym for the word *shiny* in the fifth sentence.

CHAPTER TWO **Nouns and Pronouns**

A noun names a person, place, or thing.

Welcome to Word Land! This is a special place where you will learn many new things about your language. During this school year you will meet some new friends: nouns, pronouns, verbs, adverbs, and adjectives. Each has a different job to do. You must learn to recognize them and to use them correctly. Make them your friends.

IDENTIFYING NOUNS

Words most often used are those that identify some person, place, or thing. Many of them, like *dentist, George,* and *girl* name persons. Others, like *park, New Jersey,* and *seashore,* name places. Some, such as *candy, television,* and *books,* name things. These words are called *nouns.*

A *noun* names a person, place, or thing.

PERSONS	PLACES	THINGS
dentist	park	candy
George	New Jersey	television
girl	seashore	books

169

EXERCISE 25

Use the following nouns to complete each sentence below:

children   teacher   Jack   doctor

1 _____is my brother.
2 The_____played at the park.
3 The_____gave me medicine for a cold.
4 Miss Young is our new_____ .

Use the following nouns to complete each sentence below:

Dallas   motel   camp   Spain

1 Columbus sailed from_____.
2 _____is a large city.
3 We learned to swim at summer_____ .
4 I stayed at a_____last night.

Use the following nouns to complete each sentence below:

flower   chair   drum   pizza

1 She sat down in the_____ .
2 He plays a_____in the school band.
3 _____is my favorite food.
4 The_____bloomed in the garden.

EXERCISE 26

Play the game "Noun Riddles." Choose a word that names a person, place, or thing. Then think of some clues to put in riddle form. Here are some sample Noun Riddles.

1 I am the name of a thing. I keep time in hours, minutes, and seconds. Often I hang on a wall. What am I?

2 I am the name of a person. My job is to fly airplanes, both large and small. Who am I?

More Work with Nouns

Sometimes people are called by names that show the kind of work they do. For example, you speak of a doctor, a painter, a pilot, or a cook. These are all names referring to *persons*. People work in the country, in an office, or in a factory. These are all the names of *places*. People may work with tools, with paints, or with food. These are names of *things*. Words that name persons, places, or things are called *nouns*. *Carpenter* and *boy* name persons; they are nouns. Because *park* names a place, it is a noun. *Pencil* names a thing, and is a noun.

EXERCISE 27

Make three columns on a sheet of paper. Print PERSONS at the top of the first column, PLACES at the top of the second, and THINGS at the top of the third. Write each of the following nouns in the proper column to show whether it names a person, place, or thing.

brother	lunch	telegram	mother	city	star
child	library	camera	magician	park	actress
classroom	Iowa	bubbles	beach	farmer	ship

EXERCISE 28

Use ten of the above nouns in sentences.

PROPER AND COMMON NOUNS

Have you noticed that some nouns, such as *Amy, Maine, Toronto,* and *Bob,* begin with a capital letter? These words are called *proper nouns.* Amy and Bob name *special* persons, Maine names a *special* state, and Toronto names a *special* city.

> A *proper noun* names a *special* person, place, or thing.
> A proper noun always begins with a capital letter.

COMMON	boy	ocean	automobile
PROPER	Louis	Atlantic	Ford

If a noun names *any one of a group* of persons, places, or things, it is called a *common noun.* Words such as girl, park, and bicycle are common nouns.

> A *common noun* names any one of a group of persons, places, or things.

PROPER NOUNS	COMMON NOUNS
Oak Street	street
Thanksgiving	holiday
Marcia	girl
Thomas Jefferson	president
Mississippi River	river
June	month
Sunday	day

EXERCISE 29

Study this list of nouns. Tell whether each is a proper noun

or a common noun. Remember that a proper noun begins
with a capital letter.

Bronx Zoo	beach	guard	Grand Canyon
moon	Indian Ocean	snake	lake
banana	fish	Jimmy	Bambi
Ohio River	camera	desert	crayon
lion	Disneyland	Elsa	Carmen

EXERCISE 30

Copy the following sentences. Draw *one* line under each
proper noun and *two* lines under each common noun.

1 Jason kicked the football.
2 The ship sailed across the ocean.
3 Don plays the trumpet.
4 Mickey Mouse is a cartoon character.
5 Todd dropped the dish.
6 The fort was made of rocks.
7 Benji is a famous dog in the movies.
8 Carol lives in England.
9 The car came slowly up the driveway.
10 Laura hurt her foot.

SINGULAR AND PLURAL NOUNS

Would you like to be a "word detective"? Look carefully at
the following sentences. Do you notice the difference between the nouns in italics?

Paul is a *boy*. There are three other *boys* in his family.
There were many *stars* in the sky, but I only wished on one
star.
On our block, three *houses* are for sale. Our *house* is not for
sale.

If you are alert, you noticed that some of the nouns ended in the letter *s*. These nouns represent *more than one*.

Boy, star, and *house* name one person or one thing. These nouns are *singular*. A *singular noun* names one person, place, or thing.

Boys, stars and *houses* name more than one person or thing. These nouns are *plural*. A *plural noun* names more than one person, place, or thing.

Forming the Plural of Nouns

Forming the plural of nouns will be easy if you study carefully these rules:

Many nouns form the plural by adding *s* to the singular.

SINGULAR (one)	PLURAL (more than one)
day	days
ocean	oceans
doll	dolls
store	stores
apple	apples
uncle	uncles
hand	hands

Nouns ending in *s, x, z, sh,* and *ch* form the plural by adding *es* to the singular.

SINGULAR (one)	PLURAL (more than one)
guess	guesses
bush	bushes
ax	axes
glass	glasses
porch	porches
fox	foxes
buzz	buzzes
peach	peaches

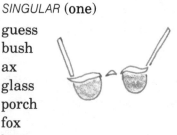

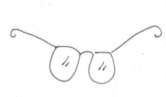

EXERCISE 31

Tell whether the following nouns are singular or plural:

bird	dresses	bear	animals
boats	lamp	shells	nurse
shoes	colors	island	cars
eye	blocks	goats	whale
rug	nest	horses	nests

EXERCISE 32

Write the plural of each of the following nouns:

dish	door	mix	class
plant	box	glove	tent
map	torch	pool	witch
inch	race	cone	bed
player	clown	watch	tree

EXERCISE 33

Copy the following sentences and tell whether the noun in italics is singular or plural:

1   The *birds* hopped quickly.
2   Name three *animals*.
3   We saw the *conductor*.
4   *Joel* called to us.
5   The *bell* sounded loud and clear.
6   The *boys* examined it.
7   The *streets* had grown dark.
8   The *jar* was difficult to open.
9   They found the lost golf *ball*.
10   I enjoy most *games*.
11   My sister knit these *mittens*.
12   The *roses* are in bloom.

NOUNS SHOW POSSESSION

Nouns are very interesting words. Already we know that nouns perform important tasks in our language. Nouns *name* persons, places, or things. Nouns may be *singular* or *plural*. But nouns do more.

Nouns show ownership or possession. To *own* a thing is to *possess* a thing. In writing, to show that a person owns or possesses something, we place an *apostrophe* (') and the letter *s* after the name of the *owner*.

Bud's sneaker	(Bud *owns* a sneaker.)
the dog's paw	(The dog *possesses* a paw.)
the girl's watch	(The girl *owns* a watch.)

EXERCISE 34

Read each pair of sentences. One sentence in each pair contains a noun that shows possession. Tell which sentence in the pair uses a possessive form.

1 a Uncle Pete has a new car.
   b Uncle Pete's car is new.

2 a The cat's fur is dark.
   b The cat has fur that is dark.

3 a A shark's teeth are sharp.
   b A shark has sharp teeth.

4 a The trophy that belongs to Nick is large.
   b Nick's trophy is large.

5 a The baby's bottle is empty.
   b The baby has an empty bottle.

6 a The bird's nest is made of twigs.
   b The nest that belongs to the bird is made of twigs.

7 a The bike has good brakes.
   b The bike's brakes are good.

EXERCISE 35

In each of the following sentences, tell which word shows possession or ownership:

1 The singer's voice was beautiful.
2 I stayed at Lucy's house last night.
3 My grandfather's garden is in bloom.
4 The boat's motor was broken.
5 We drank the cow's milk.
6 Sherri's ring was lost on her class trip.
7 The dog's bowl is empty.
8 My father's tools are very valuable.
9 The child's toy is made of plastic.
10 The girl's jacket hung in the closet.

EXERCISE 36

Write each of the following groups of words to show possession.

EXAMPLE: the eyes of the tiger—the *tiger's* eyes

1 the music of the band
2 the cage of the monkey
3 the stem of the flower
4 the hat of Debby
5 the hockey stick of Gary
6 the name of the doctor
7 the brush of the painter
8 the wheel of the truck
9 the wings of the airplane
10 the suit of Don

Singular Possessives

A singular noun may name *one* person, *one* place, or *one* thing. When a singular noun shows ownership, we add an *apostrophe* and *s* to the noun.

EXAMPLES

the horse of my *friend* (*one* friend)   my *friend's* horse

the drill of the *worker* (*one* worker)   the *worker's* drill

the pages of the *book* (*one* book)   the *book's* pages

SINGULAR NOUN	POSSESSIVE FORM
friend	friend's
worker	worker's
book	book's

EXERCISE 37

Complete the following sentences. Make the singular noun at the left show ownership, and fill in each blank correctly.

Elaine	1	We went to _____ birthday party.
jockey	2	The _____ horse was led around the ring.
skunk	3	A _____ fur is black and white.
picture	4	The _____ frame was painted gold.
catcher	5	A _____ mitt is heavily padded.
Joyce	6	_____ hair is black.
camera	7	Look through the _____ lens.
neighbor	8	The pile of rocks blocked our _____ driveway.
king	9	We saw a _____ crown in the museum.
tree	10	The _____ leaves are falling.

EXERCISE 38

The apostrophe has been omitted in each of the following word groups. Rewrite each to show that *one* person or thing is the owner.

1 my aunts pies
2 Teds motorcycle
3 the dancers costume
4 Glorias necklace
5 The boys shirt

6 the lions den
7 my brothers apartment
8 the guides name
9 Julias pool
10 the chickens wing

Plural Possessives

A plural noun names *more than one* person, place, or thing. If one girl is riding her bicycle and another girl joins her, we say there are two girls *(girls* is a plural noun). If we write about the *bicycles* these girls are riding, we write *the girls' bicycles.* We form the possessive of a plural noun ending in *s* by adding only the apostrophe after the *s.*

Words meaning more than one, ending in *s*, add only an apostrophe to show possession.

EXAMPLES

the pen of the *pigs*
   (more than one pig)
the lockers of the *players*
   (more than one player)
the answers of the *students*
   (more than one student)

the *pigs'* pen

the *players'* lockers

the *students'* answers

SINGULAR	PLURAL	POSSESSIVE FORM
pig	pigs	pigs'
player	players	players'
student	students	students'

Other words that refer to more than one person, place, or thing do not end in *s*. One man parks his car in the lot. If another man pulls up beside him, we say there are two *men* parking cars *(men* is a plural noun). If we write about the *cars* these men are parking, we write *the men's cars.* The plural of *man* is *men,* so we add an *apostrophe* and *s* to show possession.

> **When plural nouns *do not* end in *s*, add an apostrophe and *s* to show possession.**

EXAMPLES

the pencils of the *children*
(more than one child)

the *children's* pencils

the shoes of the *women*
(more than one woman)

the *women's* shoes

the tails of the *mice*
(more than one mouse)

the *mice's* tails

SINGULAR	*PLURAL*	*POSSESSIVE FORM*
child	children	children's
woman	women	women's
mouse	mice	mice's

EXERCISE 39

Complete the following sentences. Make the plural noun at the left show ownership, and fill in each blank correctly.

players	1	The _____ uniforms are green and white.
childrens	2	All the _____ toys were collected.
Indians	3	The _____ pottery was on display at the mall.
coaches	4	Are the _____ teams ready for the tournament?
sisters	5	My _____ jobs take them all over the country.
mice	6	_____ tails are long, narrow, and almost hairless.
scientists	7	The _____ laboratories were locked.
girls	8	Were you invited to the _____ party?
clowns	9	The _____ faces were funny.
thrushes	10	The _____ songs filled the air.

EXERCISE 40

The apostrophe has been omitted in each of the following word groups. Rewrite each to show that *more than one* person or thing is the owner.

1 the chickens feathers
2 many cooks aprons
3 the captains ships
4 some settlers cabins
5 the nurses uniforms
6 the mens ties
7 all students projects
8 the elephants trunks
9 our teachers desks
10 the hens eggs

NOUN SUBSTITUTES: PRONOUNS

Now you are ready to meet another group of word friends. These words are called *pronouns*. They take the place of nouns in sentences. Here are some pronouns:

I, we	you	he, she, it, they
mine, ours	yours	his, hers, its, theirs
me, us	you	him, her, it, them

Read the following poem about a boy named Jim and his mother. Notice how the author, Gwendolyn Brooks, uses noun substitutes. Can you tell what nouns the italicized words represent?

JIM
by Gwendolyn Brooks

There never was a nicer boy
Than Mrs. Jackson's Jim.
The sun should drop *its* greatest gold
On *him*.

Because, when Mother-dear was sick,
He brought *her* cocoa in.
And brought *her* broth, and brought *her* bread,
And brought *her* medicine.

And, tipping, tidied up *her* room.
And would not let *her* see
He missed *his* game of baseball
Terribly.

The words *he, him,* and *his* are substitutes for the noun Jim. The word *her* takes the place of the noun Mother('s). The word *its* stands for sun's.

> **A pronoun is a word used in place of a noun. The work of a pronoun is *to take the place of the noun.***

EXERCISE 41

Find the pronouns in each of the following sentences:

1 We paddled the canoe.
2 The thunder scared us.
3 You must speak louder.
4 That van in the driveway is ours.
5 She walked on the balance beam.
6 Give the library card to him.
7 I took a trip to Hawaii.
8 What is Karen going to do with hers?
9 They looked for shells on the beach.
10 The judge awarded the prize to me.

EXERCISE 42

In each of the following sentences, write a pronoun to take the place of the italicized noun:

1 The *children* went to the amusement park.
2 *Lee* runs very fast.

continued on next page

3 The *girl* boarded the bus for school.
4 He painted the *house*.
5 The *car* always stalls.
6 Give the report to *Meg*.
7 Invite *Ed* to dinner.
8 The *kittens* purred softly.
9 *Grace* plays the piano.
10 *Marty* is moving today.

Pronouns at Work

Good writers always look for ways to make their work better. They know that sentences often become boring when nouns are repeated. Pronouns, or noun substitutes, can be used to improve sentences. Notice how this writer made good use of pronouns to improve his sentences:

FIRST DRAFT

Greg went to the store for his mother. Greg's mother gave Greg a list and some money. When Greg returned with the items, Greg gave Greg's mother the change.

IMPROVED (with pronouns)

Greg went to the store for his mother. *She* gave *him* a list and some money. When *he* returned with the items, *he* gave *her* the change.

EXERCISE 43

Rewrite the following sentences using pronouns to take the place of the nouns in italics:

1   Beth's aunt bought *Beth* a new coat.
2   Give Paul's book to *Paul*.
3   Jack and Lou flew the plane. *Jack and Lou* are good pilots.
4   The lawnmower is old. *The lawnmower* needs new parts.
5   Sam called for help. *Sam* shouted and shouted.
6   Take Mike and John's baseballs to *Mike and John*.
7   Sally broke a window. *Sally* reported the accident.
8   Dave was walking *Dave's* dog.
9   Sue and Tina go surfing. *Sue and Tina* like to ride big waves.
10 Kathy celebrated a birthday. *Kathy* is ten years old.

EXERCISE 44

When the author wrote this paragraph, he used the same nouns again and again. Can you improve the sentences by using pronouns in place of the nouns?

Jill's brother, Tom, would not let Jill ride a skateboard. Jill was too little and Tom was afraid Jill would get hurt. Tom explained this to Jill so that Jill would understand.

Using Pronouns Correctly

When we speak, we imitate language patterns. We hear our parents, brothers, sisters, neighbors, and friends speak. We try to copy what they say. If they are speaking correct English, we learn correct language patterns.

Sometimes young children "jumble" language patterns they hear. For example:

INCORRECT LANGUAGE PATTERN: "Me want a drink of water."
CORRECT LANGUAGE PATTERN: "I want a drink of water."

Read the following sentences. Listen for the pronoun *I* in the correct language pattern.

I picked a basket of apples.
My brother and *I* are going to camp.
It was *I* at the door.
I grew two inches this year.
Roberto and *I* are good friends.

BE POLITE

When you tell what you do
With others, please try
To put yourself last
And call yourself *I*.

Read the following sentences. Listen carefully for the pronoun *me* in the correct language pattern.

Please give *me* a soda.
The stone hit *me* in the leg.
He gave free tickets to Julie and *me*.
"Clear the table for *me*," said Grandmother.
Amy called *me* on the telephone.

EXERCISE 45

Read each sentence aloud. Tell why *I* comes after the other person's name.

1 Pete and I always help the teacher.
2 David and I went to the game.
3 My brother and I like cookies.
4 Ellen and I washed the dishes.
5 Yesterday, Uncle Rob and I caught a big fish.
6 Mother and I went to the store.
7 Ed and I saw the parade.
8 Mary Jane and I are friends.
9 He and I are going to school.
10 Steve and I built a snowman.

Remember that the word *I* is always written with a capital letter.

EXERCISE 46

Read the following sentences. Decide if the pronoun *I* or the pronoun *me* is correct in the language pattern.

1 (I, Me) received my report card.
2 Please take (I, me) to the carnival.
3 Danny went to the game with Patti and (I, me).
4 Show (I, me) your notebook, please.
5 From the airplane, (I, me) saw the clouds.
6 (I, Me) caught a large fish.
7 Lois bought an ice cream cone for (I, me).
8 (I, Me) like to play kickball.
9 Am (I, me) in first place?
10 Rita saw (I, me) at the station.

EXERCISE 47

Copy the following sentences. Fill in the blanks with the pronoun *I* or *me*. Be careful to follow the correct language patterns.

1 _____ lost my umbrella.
2 My mother and _____ enjoy baking cookies.
3 These boots do not fit _____ .
4 _____ attended my first ice hockey game.
5 He passed the basketball to _____ .
6 The captain and _____ lifted the sail.
7 _____ held the soft, furry rabbit.
8 _____ swam across the pool.
9 Pass the food to Harry and _____ .
10 Bring your test paper to _____ .

WORD STUDY

Dictionary Skills

In Chapter One you took a walk down Alphabet Lane, where you met the word wizard, the dictionary. In this chapter, you will become better acquainted with the dictionary.

The dictionary is a book containing words arranged in alphabetical order. Each word listed in a dictionary is called an *entry word*. The entry word is followed by directions for pronunciation and the meanings of the word.

Getting to know the dictionary is a simple task, because it is divided into three sections: the beginning, the middle, and the end. In these sections the letters of the alphabet are grouped like this:

BEGINNING	MIDDLE	END
a b c d e f g h i	j k l m n o p q	r s t u v w x y z

If you remember the three sections, you will be able to locate entry words quickly, and be on your way to becoming a "word wizard," too.

EXERCISE 48

Write *beginning, middle,* or *end* after each of these words to show in what part of the dictionary you will find it:

flag	rash	hive	scout
parade	blizzard	whale	patio
jersey	dragon	thorn	locker

EXERCISE 49

Write the headings *Beginning, Middle,* and *End* in three columns at the top of your paper, then arrange the words in each numbered line according to the proper dictionary sections:

EXAMPLE: arch, shadow, nightmare

Beginning	*Middle*	*End*
arch	nightmare	shadow

1 book, today, lemon
2 unlock, curve, paddle
3 vase, meter, Eskimo
4 lamb, tugboat, bubble
5 dentist, wigwam, jungle
6 footprint, yellow, orange
7 zero, goose, know
8 queen, muffin, infant

Synonyms

Words are somewhat like athletes. A player often gets tired while playing in a game on the field, court, or track. Then the coach sends in a substitute for him. Words, too, are overworked in sentences. They can be replaced with other words that mean the same or nearly the same. These words are called *synonyms*. Look at the overworked word in the following sentence:

Jane is a *happy* girl.

The word *happy* could use a replacement. It is used too frequently, and becomes overworked. We could use the words *cheerful, glad,* or *joyful* instead. They mean the same,

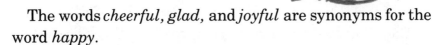

or nearly the same, as the word happy.

> Jane is a *cheerful* girl.
> Jane is a *glad* girl.
> Jane is a *joyful* girl.

The words *cheerful, glad,* and *joyful* are synonyms for the word *happy*.

> **Synonyms are words of nearly the same meaning.**

EXERCISE 50

Match the word in Column A with a synonym in Column B.

COLUMN A	COLUMN B
talk	gift
pal	bring
present	friend
carry	speak

EXERCISE 51

Using the synonyms in the exercise above, complete the following sentences:

1 _____ that magazine to me, please.
2 Vince is a _____ of mine.
3 I left the wedding _____ on the table.
4 At dinner, all of us get a chance to _____.
5 Will you help me to _____ this typewriter.
6 The _____ was wrapped in blue paper with an orange bow.
7 Try to _____ in a loud, clear voice.
8 Terri is my _____ because we play well together.

Antonyms

In Word Land there once lived a giant and a dwarf. The giant's name was *First*. He was very proud, and liked to lead all the processions. The dwarf, whose name was *Last,* was very timid. He was always the last person to fall in line.

The giant and the dwarf are opposites. Why? The words *first* and *last* are also opposites. They have opposite meanings. Words of opposite meaning are called *antonyms*.

> The giant was the *first* person in the parade.
> The dwarf was the *last* person in the parade.

Antonyms are words that are opposite in meaning.

EXERCISE 52

Read the following sentences. Write the opposite of the word printed in italics in the blanks.

1 December is the *last* month of the year. January is the _____ month.
2 Susan arrived *first,* and Marie came _____.
3 I brush my teeth *first* thing in the morning and _____ thing in the evening.
4 In the race Louis came in *first* and David came in _____.
5 Saturday is the *last* day of the week and Sunday is the _____ day.
6 Were you the *first* boy in line or the _____ boy?
7 I live in the *last* house on the street and my cousin lives in the _____ house.
8 The *first* answer on your paper is right, but the _____ one is wrong.

Homonyms

Homonyms are another special group of words. Homonyms are words that sound alike, but are not spelled alike, and do not have the same meaning.

In this lesson you will meet three sets of homonyms: *dear* and *deer, meat* and *meet, ate* and *eight.*

"DEAR" and "DEER"

When we wrote our letters of invitation, we greeted our friends by saying "Dear_____ ." The word *dear* is an expression of affection.

Another word that sounds like *dear* is *deer*. The word *deer* is the name of an animal that lives in the forest. See how these two homonyms are used in sentences:

He is a *dear* little boy.
A female *deer* is called a doe.

If we are writing about an animal, we use the word *deer*. This word has two *e*'s. If we write about someone we love, we use the word *dear*. This word has one *e* and one *a*.

Homonyms are words that sound alike, but are not spelled alike, and do not have the same meaning.

EXERCISE 53

Copy the following sentences. Write the correct word, *dear* or *deer*, in each of the blank spaces.

1 We saw a _____ at the zoo.
2 _____ Peggy, please come soon.
3 We should be kind to our _____ parents.
4 Many _____ roam the forest.
5 Mrs. Wilson was a _____ friend of my mother.
6 My father likes to hunt _____ .
7 The horns of the _____ are long.
8 In her letter she wrote, "_____ Patricia."
9 Some people eat _____ meat.
10 My mother is a very _____ to me.
11 An elk is a large _____ .
12 I have a _____ little sister.

"MEAT" and "MEET"

When someone is introduced to us, we usually say, "I am happy to *meet* you." The word *meet* means "to make the acquaintance of." Another word which sounds like *meet* is *meat*. This means a food we eat. See how they are used in sentences:

> I will *meet* you at the corner.
> *Meat* is an important part of our diet.

EXERCISE 54

Copy the following sentences. Write the correct word, *meat* or *meet,* in each of the blank spaces.

1 _____ me at the train.
2 Pork is _____ .
3 Rich was pleased to _____ you.
4 The club will _____ this afternoon.
5 Jim bought some _____ .
6 The team ran to _____ their coach.
7 This package of _____ is heavy.
8 We _____ many friends at school.
9 Too much _____ is not good for children.
10 Where did you _____ your friends?

"ATE" and "EIGHT"

In one of the letters you copied, you wrote that the plane left New York "at eight o'clock." *Eight* is another way of writing the number 8. This word has a sound twin, *ate*. *Ate* is the past tense of *eat*.

There are *eight* pumpkins in the contest.

Wendy *ate* all the vegetables on her plate.

EXERCISE 55

Copy the following sentences. Choose the correct word from the words in parentheses.

1 Six and two are (eight, ate).
2 The children (eight, ate) too much candy.
3 Joe (eight, ate) the ice cream quickly.
4 Four times two equals (eight, ate).
5 The monkey at the zoo (eight, ate) the peanuts.
6 We begin school at (eight, ate) o'clock.
7 Peter solved (eight, ate) problems.
8 We (eight, ate) popcorn at the movies.
9 (Eight, Ate) boys and girls went to the party.
10 The hungry children (eight, ate) sandwiches.

Contractions

"DIDN'T"

We often take short cuts to make our speaking and writing easier. We can take a short cut by writing the words *did* and *not* together, and omitting the letter *o*. We put an apostrophe above the place where the *o* is left out. Our short cut is *didn't*.

WORDS	CONTRACTION	CHANGES
did not	didn't	Take out the *o*.
		Put in the apostrophe (').

The pilot *didn't* receive the message.

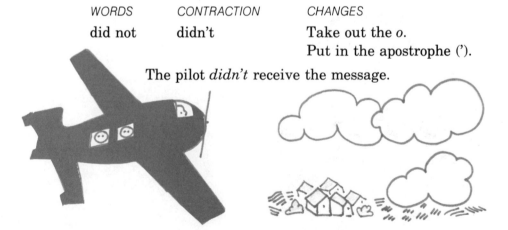

EXERCISE 56

In each of the following sentences change the words *did not* to *didn't*:

1 Christopher Columbus did not know he had discovered a new land.
2 The acrobat did not complete his act.
3 I did not see you on the bus.
4 The snow did not last long.
5 Juan did not read that story.
6 The poor old woman did not know what to do.
7 Peter did not let the water come through the dike.
8 The baby slipped, but he did not fall.
9 My sister did not mail the letter.
10 The thunder and lightning did not frighten the small children.

"WASN'T" and "WEREN'T"

When the word *not* is joined to the word *was,* we form the contraction *wasn't.* When these two words are written as one, the *o* drops out and the apostrophe takes its place.

Another contraction is made by writing *were* and *not* as the word *weren't.* In this word, too, the apostrophe takes the place of the letter *o* in *not.*

WORDS	CONTRACTION	CHANGES
was not	wasn't	Take out the *o*.
		Put in the apostrophe (')·
were not	weren't	Take out the *o*.
		Put in the apostrophe (')·

Your name *wasn't* on the list.
Judy's books *weren't* in the desk.

Wasn't is used when we speak of *one* person, place, or thing.

Weren't is used when we speak of *more than one* person, place, or thing, and with the pronoun *you* whether it means *one* or *more than one*.

EXERCISE 57

Copy each of the following sentences. Use contractions in place of the words printed in italics.

1 It *was not* he.
2 You *were not* on time.
3 I *was not* at the baseball park yesterday.
4 The boys *were not* on that train.
5 You *were not* at home when I called.
6 The alarm clock *was not* working.
7 Pierre's bicycle *was not* in the yard.
8 Susan and Leslie *were not* at the party.
9 The bread *was not* on the table.
10 The shepherd *was not* watching the sheep.
11 Brother Fox and Brother Rabbit *were not* friends.
12 The skates *were not* in the closet.
13 Why *were not* the children at school?
14 Badminton *was not* a hard game to learn.

EXERCISE 58 [Chapter Challenge]

Read this paragraph orally and then copy on paper the sentences that follow it. Fill in the blanks for a self-check on what you have learned in this chapter.

WATCHING THE PARADE

¹Sam watched the parade while sitting on his father's shoulders. ²From that special seat, he counted eight brightly colored floats. ³The bands that passed by came all the way from the state of New York. ⁴A drill team marched last in the parade. ⁵Sam was disappointed because they didn't perform for the crowd. ⁶How he wished the parade had ended on a more exciting note!

1 _____ is the proper noun in sentence one.
2 The noun in sentence one that shows ownership or possession is _____ .
3 In the first sentence *shoulders* means more than one. It is a _____ noun.
4 The pronoun in sentence two that takes the place of the noun *Sam* is _____ .
5 Give a homonym for the word *eight* in sentence two. _____ .
6 A common noun in sentence two is _____ .
7 In sentence three *state* is a common noun and _____ is a proper noun.
8 Name an antonym for the word *last* in sentence four. _____ .
9 In sentence five, *didn't* is a contraction for _____ .
10 The pronoun *they* in sentence five is a substitute for _____ in sentence four.
11 _____ is the pronoun in sentence six.
12 *Parade* in sentence six is a _____ _____ .

CHAPTER THREE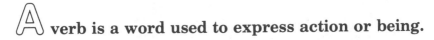

A verb is a word used to express action or being.

The boys and girls in Wordland were having a "Show and Tell" period at school. Tim brought his pet hamster in a cage. This is what he told the class:

> My hamster always *plays* with me.
> He *jumps* and *turns,* as you can see.
> He *chews* his food without a sound.
> Then *swings* the wheel round and round.

The italicized words that tell what Tim's hamster does are called action words or *verbs.* Can you think of other verbs to tell what a hamster can do? We use many verbs in speaking and in writing. Every sentence must contain a verb.

A *verb* is a word used to express action or being.

ACTION VERBS—express action.   Rita *hurried* to the store.
BEING VERBS—express being.   Rita *is* my sister.

ACTION VERBS

Most verbs express action. The verbs you will study first are *action verbs.* An action verb tells something that the sub-

201

ject of the sentence *does* or *did*.

> Janet *watches* television.
> The little boy *opened* the cookie jar.
> The wind *blew* down that sign.

The words in italics are action verbs.

EXERCISE 59

Read this poem and answer the questions that follow:

HOW CREATURES MOVE

The lion walks on padded paws,
The squirrel leaps from limb to limb,
While flies can crawl straight up a wall
And seals can dive and swim.
The worm he wiggles all around,
The monkey swings by his tail;
And birds may hop upon the ground
Or spread their wings and sail.
But boys and girls
Have much more fun:
They leap and dance
And walk and run.

—Unknown

1   How does the lion move?
2   What action does the squirrel do?
3   Name the creatures that can *crawl*.
4   What creature can *dive* and *swim?*
5   How does the worm move?
6   What creatures *hop, spread,* and *sail?*
7   What is the action of the monkey?
8   Who can *leap, dance, walk,* and *run?*
9   Do all the creatures move in the same manner?
10   What part of speech denotes action?

EXERCISE 60

Name the action verbs in the following sentences:

1 The jet flew through the clouds.
2 The children laughed at the funny story.
3 The dog barked at the man.
4 My father works in a factory downtown.
5 Spiders spin webs.
6 The wild mustangs galloped across the prairie.
7 Barbara read four books last month.
8 I called my friend on the telephone.
9 He dove off the raft.
10 Sara pulled down the shade.
11 Our class visited the art museum.
12 Who rang the doorbell?
13 The president talked on T.V. last night.
14 Amy swims every day in the pool.

EXERCISE 61

Copy the following nouns. Write three action verbs that could be used with these nouns.

airplane	___	___	___
coach	___	___	___
Mark	___	___	___
monkey	___	___	___
band	___	___	___

EXERCISE 62

Write three *original* sentences using some of the nouns and verbs in Exercise 61. Underline the action verbs in your sentences.

BEING VERBS

Not all verbs express action. Some verbs express being. The following are *being verbs:*

is (am)	was	has been
are	were	have been
		had been

Read these sentences:

Tyrone *plays* football.	(action)
Tyrone *is* a football player.	(being)

In the first sentence the verb *plays* is an action verb. It tells something Tyrone *does*. In the second sentence, the verb simply expresses *being*. It is a *verb of being*.

EXERCISE 63

Copy the following sentences, filling each blank with an action or being verb as noted. Being verbs can be found in the list above.

1 The children_____ an unusual shell on the beach.
       (action)
2 Bugs Bunny_____ a funny cartoon character.
       (being)
3 Daffodils_____ beautiful flowers.
     (being)
4 The huge rock_____ onto the road.
      (action)
5 This book_____ exciting.
     (being)
6 Daniel Boone_____ a brave pioneer.
      (being)

7 Steve_____ a game of ping-pong.
      (action)
8 My brother_____ a dentist.
            (being)
9 Francisco_____ a letter to his friend.
            (action)
10 The movie_____ frightening.
            (being)

FORMS OF VERBS

Every verb has three basic forms: present, past, and past participle.

PRESENT	Tells about something *happening now*.
PAST	Tells about something that *has happened*.
PAST PARTICIPLE	Is used with a helper. Some of its helpers are *have, has,* and *had*.

PRESENT	PAST	PAST PARTICIPLE (helper)
play	played	has played

EXERCISE 64

Tell what form of the verb—present, past, past participle—is used in each of the following sentences:

1 The children *played* hockey at Baker field.
2 Fred *works* in a supermarket.
3 The robot *moved* across the room.
4 I *had baked* cookies many times before.
5 I *looked* everywhere for my roller skates.
6 My dog *follows* me to school.
7 The crowd *clapped* loudly for the band.
8 The firefighter *crawled* along the ledge.

continued on next page

9 The soldiers *march* every day.
10 The farmers *have planted* many watermelon seeds.
11 The little boy *filled* the bucket with sand.
12 We *rowed* to the other side of the lake.

EXERCISE 65

Copy the following chart, filling in the missing parts of the verb:

	PRESENT	*PAST*	*PAST PARTICIPLE*
1	watch		
2		raked	
3			had climbed
4		cheered	
5	jump		
6	tape		
7	chase		
8			has received
9		helped	
10	jog		

Regular and Irregular Verbs

Read aloud the list of verbs in Exercise 65. All these verbs form their past and past participle by adding *d* or *ed* to the present tense. They are called *regular* verbs. Some verbs do *not* form their past and past participle by adding *d* or *ed*. These are called *irregular* verbs.

Read these sentences:

Every day I *go* to school.
Last year I *went* to the Virgin Islands.
I *have gone* to this restaurant many times before.

The verb *go* is an irregular verb. The past form of *go* is *went*. The past participle is *gone*. Notice the verb *gone* has a helping verb. The past participle always takes a helping verb.

Study this list of irregular verbs.

PRESENT	PAST	PAST PARTICIPLE (helper)
bring	brought	brought
buy	bought	bought
come	came	come
do	did	done
eat	ate	eaten
give	gave	given
go	went	gone
is (am)	was (were)	been
run	ran	run
see	saw	seen
sit	sat	sat
take	took	taken
tear	tore	torn
write	wrote	written

The third part of the verb, the past participle, must be used with a helper or auxiliary verb. Some of these words are *is, are, was, were, has, had,* or *have.*

Drill on Irregular Verb Forms

"BRING," "BROUGHT," "BROUGHT"

Bring is used to tell about something that is happening now.

> *Bring* your paper to me.

When we wish to tell something that has happened in the past, we use *brought*.

Carol and Rosa *brought* gifts to Steve and Susan.
I *brought* my drawing home.

The third part of the verb, *brought*, must be used with a helper, such as *has, had, have, is, are, was,* or *were*.

David and Laura *have brought* their roller skates.
Paul *has brought* his stamp collection.
He *had brought* it yesterday.

EXERCISE 66

Copy the following sentences. Write the correct form, *bring* or *brought,* in each blank space.

1 The messenger _____ the telegram.
2 We _____ our lunch to school every day.
3 They _____ this rug from the attic.
4 Elizabeth, please _____ my mail.
5 Dennis has _____ his softball to school.
6 The class _____ pictures for the bulletin board.
7 _____ me the newspaper, Donald.
8 Has Dave _____ his camera?
9 Farmers _____ fresh vegetables to the city every morning.
10 The astronauts had _____ their equipment with them.

"BUY," "BOUGHT,""BOUGHT"

The word *buy* means to purchase.
Buy tells about something that is happening now.

> Please *buy* a ticket for our play.

Bought tells of something that has happened in the past.

> I *bought* a coloring book for my brother.

The past participle, *bought,* must be used with a helper such as *have, has, had, is, are, was,* or *were.*

> Mother *has bought* all her gifts.

EXERCISE 67

Copy the following sentences. Fill in each blank with *buy* or *bought.*

1 Mother _____ fresh eggs at the farm stand.
2 The children _____ milk every day.
3 Our class has _____ a gerbil.
4 Where is the basket which I _____ yesterday?
5 The boys have _____ a new basketball.
6 I have just _____ a red pen.
7 Mother, please _____ me an ice-cream cone.
8 Marge _____ a box of candy for her teacher.
9 He had _____ a bicycle with the money he saved.
10 They _____ hamburgers for lunch.
11 We _____ meat in the butcher shop.
12 What gift have you _____ for your mother?
13 _____ fresh fruit here.
14 The Mayers have _____ a new home on Lexington Avenue.

"COME," "CAME," "COME"

Come is used to tell about something that is happening now.

> *Come* with me, please.

When we tell about something that happened in the past, we use *came*.

> Yesterday, he *came* to our house.

Come may be used with the helpers *has, have,* and *had.*

> Bruce *has come* with us every time.

EXERCISE 68

Copy the following sentences. Fill each blank with *come* or *came*.

1 Jerome _____ to see the play last night.
2 Our class has _____ to this museum before.
3 Ruth, _____ over and play with our video game.
4 Six judges _____ for the science fair.
5 Who has _____ for the package?
6 _____ every day, and you will receive a prize.
7 The books _____ last week.
8 Has the train _____ yet?
9 "_____ and see for yourself," said the salesman.
10 Betty _____ to see her brother perform.
11 A nice breeze _____ from the fan.
12 We _____ to buy some goldfish.
13 Julie has _____ before, but you were not here.
14 _____ now, before the crowd gets here.

"EAT," "ATE," "EATEN"

The word *eat* is used to tell about something that is happening now.

Cows *eat* grass.

The word *ate* is used to tell about something that happened in the past.

The mouse *ate* all the cheese.

With the word *eaten* we must have a helper such as *have, has, had, is, are, was,* or *were.*

William *has eaten* his spinach.

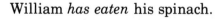

EXERCISE 69

Copy the following sentences. Write the correct form, *eat,*
ate, or *eaten,* in each blank space.

1 June _____ yogurt for lunch.
2 Ann had _____ her breakfast before I left.
3 We _____ three meals every day.
4 Yesterday they _____ their lunch at twelve o'clock.
5 _____ slowly.
6 Have you _____ the licorice?
7 Edward had _____ the apple before dinner.
8 Who _____ the ice cream?
9 Frogs and turtles _____ small insects.
10 Babies _____ soft foods.
11 _____ fresh vegetables every day.
12 The fish _____ the worm.
13 The fox _____ the grapes.
14 Have you ever _____ peach cake?
15 _____ healthful foods.
16 I _____ bread at every meal.
17 The birds had _____ the crumbs in a short time.
18 Has Bob _____ his peas?
19 The boys have _____ all the pie.
20 We _____ to live.

"GO," "WENT," "GONE"

The word *go* is used to tell something that is happening
now.

I *go* to school every day.

Went is used to tell about something that happened in the
past.

I *went* to school yesterday.

Gone is always used with a helper such as *has, had, have, is, are, was,* or *were.*

I *have gone* to school every day this week.

EXERCISE 70

Copy these sentences. Choose the correct word, *go, went,* or *gone,* in each sentence.

1 Wild geese (go, went, gone) south in winter.
2 The entire family (go, went, gone) to Florida.
3 (Go, went, gone) and clean up your room.
4 Jeff has (go, went, gone) to the post office with the letter.
5 Cinderella (go, went, gone) to the ball in a pumpkin coach.
6 The girls have (go, went, gone) sailing.
7 I (go, went, gone) to the movies every Saturday.
8 Father had (go, went, gone) to work early.
9 Barry (go, went, gone) to the pool with his brother.
10 They (go, went, gone) fishing).
11 Who (go, went, gone) to the concert with Leo?
12 Had they (go, went, gone) before you arrived?
13 The boys (go, went, gone) to the baseball game.

"SEE," "SAW," "SEEN"

The word *see* is used to tell about something that is happening now.

I *see* many toys in the window.

The word *saw* is used to tell about something that happened in the past.

I *saw* the parade yesterday.

The word *seen* must be used with the helpers *have, has,* or *had.*

I *have seen* Henry's new watch.

EXERCISE 71

Use the correct form, *see, saw,* or *seen,* in each of these sentences.

1 I_____ much better with my new glasses.
2 Have you _____ my colored pens anywhere?
3 After the storm I _____ a rainbow in the sky.
4 Have you _____ Mary?
5 My father has _____ the Amazon River.
6 They_____ a black snake in the woods.
7 It was the biggest snake they had ever_____ .
8 Mother_____ a famous actor.
9 The driver followed the signs that he_____ along the road.
10 Have you ever_____ a giraffe?
11 The children had never_____ a gorilla before.
12 We _____ many interesting machines when we toured the factory.
13 We never_____ that show anymore.

"TAKE," "TOOK," "TAKEN"

The word *take* is used to tell about something that is happening now.

Please *take* these clothes to the dry cleaner.

Took tells about something that happened in the past.

The ambulance *took* the man to the hospital.

Taken is used with a helper such as *have, has, had, is, are, was,* or *were.*

> He *has taken* the letter with him.
> They *have taken* the dog to a kennel.
> Earlier they *had taken* him for a walk.

EXERCISE 72

Copy the sentences that follow. Write the correct form, *take, took,* or *taken,* in each blank space.

1 The children have _____ the cookies to school.
2 Peggy, _____ off your coat.
3 My sister _____ a long trip on a boat.
4 _____ proper care of your teeth.
5 Has Kevin _____ his little brother to the playground?
6 We had _____ down the decorations before he came back.
7 Please _____ my picture, Mother.
8 The little boy _____ the medicine without complaining.
9 I _____ good care of my room.
10 Father _____ the car to the service station.
11 He has _____ his umbrella with him.
12 _____ your binoculars with you on the field trip.
13 _____ your sweater with you.
14 He _____ a walk through the woods.

"TEAR," "TORE," "TORN"

The word *tear* is used to tell about something that is happening now.

> Michael, *tear* the cloth into three pieces.

Tore tells about something that happened in the past.

He *tore* the paper bag on his way home.

Torn is used with a helper such as *have, has, had, is, are, was,* or *were.*

You *have torn* your jeans.
Who *has torn* the envelope?
He *had torn* the note into small pieces.

EXERCISE 73

Copy these sentences. Fill in each blank with *tear, tore,* or *torn.*

1 Who has _____ your sweater?
2 We_____ the rags to make a tail for our kite.
3 I_____ it myself.
4 Ruth has _____ the bedspread.
5 Leonard, please_____ the label off this can.
6 The wind _____ some shingles off the roof.
7 Monica has _____ her dress on this nail.
8 My little brother_____ the newspaper.
9 When he moved the piano, he_____ the rug.
10 The kitten has _____ the lace tablecloth.
11 The baby had _____ the book before I could take it away.
12 Last week the men _____ down the old building.

"SIT," "SAT," "SAT"

The word *sit* is used to tell about something that is happening now.

Steve and Susan *sit* next to each other.

Sat is used to tell about something that happened in the past.

We *sat* in a circle for our story hour yesterday.

The past participle, *sat,* must be used with a helper such as *have, has, had, is, are, was,* or, *were.*

Grandmother *has sat* in that chair for two hours.

EXERCISE 74

Copy the following sentences. Write the correct word, *sit,* or *sat,* in each blank space.

1 Mother _____ in the driver's seat.
2 Please _____ in the easy chair, Grandmother.
3 The people had _____ on the beach all day.
4 Has the little boy _____ in that chair before?
5 Humpty Dumpty _____ on the wall.
6 Where have you _____ for the last hour?
7 Go and _____ in the rocker.
8 The small child _____ on his mother's knees.
9 I _____ behind Virginia.
10 He _____ for a long time, listening to the radio.
11 On the branch of the tree _____ three little robins.
12 _____ where you _____ yesterday.
13 The dog _____ by his master's side.
14 Little Jack Horner _____ in the corner.

"WRITE," "WROTE," "WRITTEN"

The word *write* is used to tell about something that is happening now.

Steve and Susan *write* carefully.

Wrote is used to tell something that happened in the past.

Patricia *wrote* to her grandmother.

Written is used with a helper, such as *has, had, have, is, are, was* or *were*.

The twins *had written* invitations for the party.

EXERCISE 75

Copy the following sentences. Use *write, wrote,* or *written* in each blank space.

1 Please _____ your name on the first line.
2 George _____ his homework neatly.
3 Always _____ the word "I" as a capital letter.
4 Yesterday I _____ a short story.
5 The campers have _____ letters to their parents.
6 That man has _____ a long poem.
7 Tom had _____ the note before he left.
8 Carlos _____ the message on a pad by the telephone.
9 Abraham Lincoln _____ his lessons on a slate.
10 The children have _____ their paragraphs.
11 You _____ well, Sandy.
12 Daniel has _____ the address on the package.
13 Dr. Seuss _____ many books.
14 I have _____ a letter to my cousin.
15 We should think before we _____ the answers.
16 Chris, _____ the Roman numeral for fourteen.

SINGULAR AND PLURAL VERBS

Did you ever visit the zoo? Did you see the things that are talked about in this poem?

FUN AT THE ZOO

A kangaroo hops in the funniest way.
The tigers growl throughout the day.
The slimy snakes crawl here and there,
While happy crowds move everywhere.

The zookeeper walks to the lions' cage,
Followed by children of every age.
Each animal grabs his food with haste;
You can be sure there's nothing to waste.

Little Joe hugs his father so tight,
While others clap with sheer delight.
When it's time to go, the children all say,
"The zoo is the place to have a fun day."

This poem contains many nouns and verbs. Look at some of them:

kangaroo hop*s* zookeeper walk*s*
tigers growl   animal grab*s*
snakes crawl   Joe hug*s*
crowds move   others clap

Notice that some verbs end in *s,* because verbs, like nouns, may be singular or plural. *Singular* nouns use the *s* form of the verb. The pronouns *he, she, it* also use the *s* form of the verb. The verb must agree with the subject of the sentence. If we were talking about more than one kangaroo, we would say *kangaroos hop.* We would *not* use the *s* form of the verb. How would the verb change if we were talking about one tiger?

EXERCISE 76

Copy the following nouns. Add a verb to the noun. Be sure it agrees in number with the noun. Tell whether the verb is singular or plural.

1	candles _____	6	mosquitoes _____
2	Greg _____	7	stars _____
3	boats _____	8	dad _____
4	eyes _____	9	balls _____
5	pencil _____	10	kite _____

EXERCISE 77

Write three original sentences using the nouns and verbs in Exercise 76.

"IS" and "ARE"

Two words used very often are *is* and *are.* When we speak of *one* person, place, or thing we use the word *is.*

Boston *is* a large city.

When we are speaking of *more than one* person, place, or thing, we use the word *are:*

The toys *are* in the cupboard.

Are is always used with the word *you,* whether *you* stands for one person or more than one person.

You *are* a good boy.   (One person.)
You *are* good boys.   (More than one.)

EXERCISE 78

Copy each of the following sentences. Fill in the blank space with the word *is* or the word *are.*

1 That man _____ my father.
2 Mrs. Miller_____ in the kitchen.
3 Steve and Susan _____ in the third grade.
4 Your hands _____very dirty.
5 You_____ late.
6 We take a nap when we _____tired.
7 My shoes_____ new.
8 _____you in the school play?
9 _____ Louise your sister?
10 _____ the puppies in their basket?

"THERE IS" and "THERE ARE"

When *there* is used to begin a sentence, we must use the correct word after it. When we speak of one person, one place, or one thing, we say *there is* or *there was*. When we speak of more than one person, place, or thing, we say *there are* or *there were*.

There is a bird in the tree.	(One bird.)
There was a bird in the tree.	(One bird.)
There are many birds in the apple tree.	(More than one bird.)
There were many birds in the apple tree.	(More than one bird.)

EXERCISE 79

Copy each of the following sentences. Use *is* or *are* correctly in each blank space.

1 There_____a flag in front of our school.
2 There_____a mobile hanging in our classroom.
3 There_____two kinds of cookies.
4 There_____twenty-six letters in the alphabet.
5 There_____a large cake in that box.
6 There_____someone at the door.
7 There_____fifty states in the United States of America.
8 There_____good stories in this book.
9 There_____twelve months in the year.
10 There_____forty children in our class.
11 There_____thirty-one days in October.
12 There_____silk flowers in that vase.
13 There_____one hundred centimeters in a meter.
14 There_____many school buses.
15 There_____seven days in a week.
16 There_____only one apple left.

EXERCISE 80

Copy each of the following sentences. use either *was* or *were* in each blank space.

1 There _____ twenty children in the class.
2 There _____ a doctor on the airplane.
3 There _____ only one glass on the table.
4 There _____ many books on the desk.
5 There _____ a large orange in the bowl.
6 There _____ some record albums on sale today.
7 There _____ ten houses in the row.
8 There _____ a large rug on the floor.
9 There _____ once a king in Denmark who was called Canute.
10 There _____ twelve eggs in the basket.
11 There _____ no room for them at the hotel.
12 There _____ many people downtown.
13 There _____ a large chair before the fireplace.
14 There _____ hundreds of cars in the parking lot.
15 There _____ tennis players already on the court.
16 There _____ a horse in the stable.
17 There _____ five pencils on the desk.
18 There _____ a large mirror on the wall.

TROUBLESOME VERBS

"SIT" and "SET"

Neil did not have a pet, so he wrote a rhyme about some frogs.

Near the pond live two green frogs,
They sit all day on mossy logs.

When he first wrote this rhyme, Neil used the word *set* instead of *sit*. Do not confuse these words. "The word *set* means to place or to put," explained Mrs. English. "The word *sit* means to rest or recline." Notice how the words *sit* and *set* are used in these sentences:

> Sit here, Aunt Lucy.   (Take or keep a seat.)
> Set the dish on the table, Denise.   (Put or place.)

The following jingle may help students to distinguish between *sit* and *set:*

> *Sit* is a verb we frequently meet;
> Its meaning—*to have or to keep a seat.*
> *Set* is the verb to be used in case
> We mean *to fix in position* or *to place.*

EXERCISE 81

Copy the following sentences. Choose the correct word, *sit* or *set,* for each blank space.

1 Sharon, _____ the cake on the table.
2 _____ the bucket in the yard.
3 I _____ in the first seat.
4 Children, _____ quietly.
5 We _____ on that bench each evening.
6 Paul, _____ the jar on the shelf.
7 Lawrence, can you see the board from where you _____ ?
8 Who _____ the broom in the corner?
9 Martin, _____, the chairs on the stage.
10 _____ next to me, Nancy.
11 They _____ the chair by the window.
12 May I please _____ here?
13 Where did you _____ the candlesticks?
14 Let me _____ near you.

"MAY" and "CAN"

One morning Susan Parker asked, "May I be the announcer when we have the broadcast, Mrs. English?" Susan used the word *may* because she was asking for permission. The word *can* expresses ability or power to do something. *Can* and *may* are used correctly in these sentences:

You *may* play baseball tomorrow.   (Permission)
My brother *can* water ski.   (Is able to)

EXERCISE 82

Copy the following sentences. In each of the blank spaces write the correct word, *may* or *can*.

1 _____ I keep this garter snake, Mother?
2 My dog _____ sit up and beg for a bone.
3 You _____ go to the puppet show this afternoon.
4 With practice we _____ win the race.
5 _____ I carry your books?
6 Walter _____ write very neatly.
7 You _____ use my typewriter.
8 _____ I take this book home tonight?
9 Peter _____ ride a ten-speed bike.
10 Airplanes _____ travel faster than automobiles.
11 Father, _____ I please go with Tony?
12 _____ you spell all the words on this page?
13 _____ you hear the speaker?
14 _____ I have a piece of pie, please?
15 Who _____ give the correct answer?

WORD STUDY

Dictionary Skills

We often meet new words in the books we read. When we meet a new word, we want to know what it means and how to pronounce it. We must use a dictionary to help us.

The dictionary gives the meaning, correct spelling, and correct pronunciation of words. Words are arranged in alphabetical order. Words beginning with *a* come first, then follow all the words beginning with *b*, then words beginning with *c*, and so on to the letter *z*. In the dictionary, the word *elf* comes before the word *food*, because *e* comes before *f* in the alphabet.

We must know the alphabet well in order to use the dictionary with ease. We will do some exercises based on the letters of the alphabet.

ARF

EXERCISE 83

Put these letters in alphabetical order:

d s m o w e b l r q z g k x p h j n

EXERCISE 84

Put these words in alphabetical order:

fox	man	church	lamp
dog	baby	penny	railroad
art	nest	wind	store
top	elf	goose	velvet*

WORDS BEGINNING WITH THE SAME LETTER

When two words begin with the same letter, they are arranged according to the second letter of the word. The word *dog* comes before *drop*, because the second letter of *dog* comes before the second letter of *drop*. In the same way, the word *band* comes before *box*, because the second letter *a* comes before *o*. The word *soldier* comes before *street* because the letter *o* comes before *t*.

EXERCISE 85

Put these words in alphabetical order according to their first letters.

clock	after	duck	jump
present	birthday	gate	shine

EXERCISE 86

Put these words in alphabetical order according to their first and second letters:

ate	among	away	age
appear	arm	alone	afraid
answer	acorn	aim	able

Synonyms

Synonyms are words of the same or nearly the same meaning. The words *large* and *huge* are synonyms.

EXERCISE 87

The list below contains synonyms. Make two columns on your paper and write the synonyms in pairs.

shop	friendly	hunting	choose
kind	select	store	searching

EXERCISE 88

Copy the following advertisement. Replace the words in boldface with synonyms from the list above.

GRAND OPENING!
VISIT OUR NEW DOWNTOWN *STORE*
FRIENDLY SALESPERSONS WILL HELP
YOU *CHOOSE* THE ITEM YOU'VE BEEN
SEARCHING FOR!

EXERCISE 89

Fill each blank orally with a synonym for the word in italics:

1   Yesterday I went to a new *store*. It was a pet_____ .
2   I am *kind* to my dog. He is very_____ with me.
3   Did you *select* a cookie? I_____ this chocolate chip one.
4   I am *hunting* for my lost keys. My brother is also_____ for them.

Antonyms

The words *careful* and *careless* are antonyms. See how they are used in these sentences:

> *Careful* children have good table manners.
> *Careless* children have bad table manners.

Antonyms are words of opposite meanings.

EXERCISE 90

Copy the following sentences. Fill in each blank space with *careful* or *careless*.

1 Be_____ ! That plate is hot.
2 A_____ child is not neat about his appearance.
3 Mike Murphy made a very_____ mistake in his arithmetic.
4 That boy with the soiled book must be very_____ .
5 _____ people do not litter.
6 Tom made a_____ study of the map.
7 A person who does not clean his teeth is_____ .
8 Be_____ when crossing the street.
9 There would be fewer accidents if drivers were more_____ .
10 _____ people always lose things.

"BEFORE" and "BEHIND"

The words *before* and *behind* are antonyms. The word *before* means *in front of*, and the word *behind* means *in back of*. See how these words are used in sentences.

> The drum major marched *before* the band.
> The lot was *behind* the school.

EXERCISE 91

Copy the following sentences. Use the word *before* or *behind* in each of the blank spaces.

1 Jack stood _____ the audience.
2 The car was pulled _____ the tow truck.
3 As the ship steamed into the harbor, the passengers saw the Statue of Liberty _____ them.
4 When we pronounce the letter *d* we place the tongue _____ the teeth.
5 The girl hid _____ the tree.
6 _____ the counter were shelves full of toys.
7 They gazed upon the high mountains which rose _____ them.
8 The teacher stood _____ the class.
9 I could not see who sat _____ me in the auditorium.
10 The little boy pulled the red wagon _____ him.

Homonyms

Steve Parker said to his friend, "There is no happiness greater than mine when my kite is pulling at the very end of the string." *There* usually means *in that place.* The word *there* is also used to begin a sentence.

The word *their* is a *homonym* for *there.* *Their* shows ownership; it means *belonging to them.*

We must learn to use *there* and *their* correctly. These words are used correctly in the following sentences:

David was not *there* at eight o-clock. (In that place. Where?)

There are six students in the contest. (To begin a sentence.)

The children gave *their* plans to the teacher. (Ownership. Whose?)

Homonyms are words that sound alike, but are not spelled alike, and do not have the same meaning.

EXERCISE 92

Copy the following sentences. Fill in each blank with *there* or *their*.

1 _____ are thirteen stripes in our flag.
2 We looked _____ before.
3 I laid it _____ myself.
4 The girls are wearing _____ new softball uniforms.
5 People should wash _____ hands before eating.
6 The birds have built a nest _____ .
7 In the spring the farmers plant _____ crops.
8 Have you seen _____ new car?
9 Children should love and obey _____ parents.
10 Three little kittens lost _____ mittens.
11 _____ was a brown pony in the parade.
12 In autumn some trees shed _____ leaves.
13 We often play _____ .
14 My father sits _____ each evening.
15 They prepared _____ lessons well.
16 One of my classmates lives _____ .
17 I did not see you _____ .
18 Those boys have lost _____ tickets.

"HERE" and "HEAR"

What two words in this sentence sound alike?

If we sit *here,* we will be able to *hear* the singer.

These words are homonyms. They sound alike, but they differ in meaning and in spelling. *Here* usually means *in this place. Hear* means *to perceive sound with our ears. Here* and *hear* are homonyms.

EXERCISE 93

Copy the following sentences. Write *hear* or *here* in each of the blank spaces.

1 Did you _____ the thunder last night?
2 _____ is the place where I was born.
3 Can you _____ me?
4 Mother likes to _____ me sing.
5 Indians once lived _____ .
6 Autumn is _____ again.
7 We could _____ someone calling us.
8 I do not intend to stay _____ .
9 _____ is your coat.
10 Do you _____ the wind?
11 I could _____ the pounding of the surf as we neared the ocean.
12 Place the cups _____ .
13 My grandfather cannot _____ very well.
14 Susan always sits _____ .

"OUR" and "HOUR"

Our and *hour* are also homonyms. *Our* means *belonging to us. Hour* means *the time of day,* or *sixty minutes.* See how these words are used in sentences:

Mr. Jacobs is *our* principal.
There are sixty minutes in an *hour.*

EXERCISE 94

Use *our* or *hour* in each of the following sentences:

1 At what_____ do you rise?
2 _____ school colors are green and white.
3 We should love and obey_____ parents.
4 You may go swimming in one_____ .
5 This is the_____ for my favorite T.V. program.
6 The train will arrive in an_____ .
7 Here is_____ apartment.
8 Have you seen_____ new ping-pong table?
9 It takes an_____ to drive to my aunt's house.
10 The_____ passed quickly.
11 I hear_____ school bell ringing.

Contractions

"WASN'T" and "WEREN'T" [Review]

We have already learned that we use the word *was* when we speak of one person, place, or thing, and *were* when we speak of more than one person, place, or thing. The same rules apply to the use of *wasn't* and *weren't*. Here we are reviewing before we learn new contractions.

Use *wasn't* when speaking of one person, place, or thing.

The car *wasn't* in the garage.   (One thing.)

Use *weren't* when speaking of more than one person, place, or thing.

My socks *weren't* in the drawer.   (More than one thing.)

Use *weren't* with the word *you,* whether one person or more than one is meant.

Weren't you late this morning?   (With the word *you.*)

WORDS	CONTRACTIONS	CHANGES
was not	wasn't	Take out the letter *o*. Put in the apostrophe (').
were not	weren't	Take out the letter *o*. Put in the apostrophe (').

EXERCISE 95

Copy each of the following sentences. Fill in the blank space with *wasn't* or *weren't*.

1 The grass _____ mowed.
2 These tomatoes _____ grown in our garden.
3 You _____ at the party yesterday.
4 Her paper_____ as neat as it should have been.
5 Lucy_____ on time for the train.
6 The crops _____ good last year.
7 There _____ too many dishes to wash.
8 The skirt I sewed_____ difficult to make.
9 Why_____ you at the corner this morning.
10 The cherries _____ ripe.
11 I _____ awake when the bell rang.
12 The key_____ the right one.
13 The film _____ very long.

"ISN'T" and "AREN'T"

The words *is not* can be shortened to *isn't,* and the words *are not* can be shortened to *aren't*. In both these contractions the letter *o* has been left out, and an apostrophe is in its place.

This *isn't* my pencil.
The boys *aren't* here.

WORDS	CONTRACTIONS	CHANGE
is not	isn't	Take out the letter *o*. Put in the apostrophe (').
are not	aren't	Take out the letter *o*. Put in the apostrophe (').

EXERCISE 96

Copy the following sentences. Use contractions for the words printed in italics.

1 The house *is not* going to be painted this year.
2 It *is not* raining.
3 Coffee and tea *are not* good for children.
4 There *are not* many eggs in the refrigerator.
5 The banks *are not* open today.
6 Their name *is not* on the door.
7 *Are not* those the White Mountains?
8 This orange *is not* sweet.
9 Dinner *is not* ready, children.
10 *Is not* Mars a planet?
11 There *are not* many jellybeans left.

Isn't and *aren't* are like *is* and *are*. When we are talking about one person, place, or thing, we use *isn't*. When we are talking about more than one person, place, or thing, we use *aren't*. We use *aren't* with the word *you*, whether it means one person or more than one person.

> Rhode Island *isn't* a large state. (One state.)
> Tomatoes *aren't* always in season. (More than one tomato.)
> *Aren't* you ready for school? (With the word *you*.)

EXERCISE 97

Copy the following sentences. Write the word *isn't* or the word *aren't* in the blank spaces.

1 This house_____ for rent.
2 Don _____ going to the carnival with us.
3 This light bulb_____very bright.
4 The photographs _____very large.

5   Fred and Alice_____ here.
6   This pay phone_____working.
7   Her work _____ finished.
8   You _____tall enough to reach that shelf.
9   Carl_____ feeling well today.
10 _____you Susan's brother?
11 The police officer_____ on the corner now.
12 These scissors _____very sharp.

EXERCISE 98   [Chapter Challenge]

Read this story carefully; then respond orally to the directions below the paragraph.

A TRIP TO DISNEYLAND

¹Last summer our family visited Disneyland. ²First, we went to our hotel and then immediately to the park. ³The tall spires of the fantasy-land castles welcomed us. ⁴A friendly Mickey Mouse waved and invited us into the wonderland of excitement. ⁵We were careful in choosing our activities for each day. ⁶Finally, a week had passed and the hour to leave was near. ⁷It was an unforgettable vacation.

1   Name the verb in the first sentence.
2   Name the principal parts of the verb in the second sentence.
3   Is the verb in the seventh sentence a verb of *action* or of *being?*
4   Name two regular verbs in the fourth sentence.
5   Spell a homonym for the word *hour* in the sixth sentence.
6   What form of the verb is *had passed* in the sixth sentence?
7   Is the verb in the third sentence *regular* or *irregular?*
8   Give an antonym for the word *careful* in the fifth sentence.
9   Name a synonym for the word *friendly* in the fourth sentence.
10 Give a synonym for the word *choosing* in the fifth sentence.

CHAPTER FOUR # Adjectives and Adverbs

An adjective is a word used to describe a noun.

MEG'S EGG

by Mary Ann Hoberman

Meg
Likes
A *reg*ular egg
Not a poached
Or a fried
But a *reg*ular egg
Not a devilled
Or coddled
Or scrambled
Or boiled
But an *egg*ular
*Meg*ular
*Reg*ular
Egg!

In "Meg's Egg", the poet tells us in a funny way how Meg feels about eggs. In writing the poem, the author has used many words that describe the noun *egg: regular, poached, fried, devilled, coddled, scrambled* and *boiled*. These words are all *adjectives*.

An adjective is a word used to describe a noun. Adjectives usually answer the question *what kind* when we are speaking about a noun. Read these sets of sentences. Notice how adjectives help to describe a picture in words.

> The lifeguard saved the child.
> The *courageous* lifeguard saved the *frightened* child.
>
> A house stood on the street.
> A *shabby, old* house stood on the *shadowy* street.
>
> Water splashed the people.
> *Icy* water splashed the *noisy* people.

In the first set of sentences, the word *courageous* tells *what kind* of lifeguard, and *frightened* tells *what kind* of child. These adjectives make the sentences more vivid and interesting. In the second and third sets of sentences, the following adjectives are used:

> *shabby, old* house   (kind of house)
> *shadowy* street   (kind of street)
> *icy* water   (kind of water)
> *noisy* people   (kind of people)

When we read stories or poetry, we read the "word pictures" another person has drawn for us. Adjectives help to make these images clear. Let's see what would happen if we decided to take all the adjectives out of a story. Read "Summer Fun" as it was originally written:

SUMMER FUN

I have *happy* memories of my *summer* days at the shore. The *bright, hot* sun shone on me at play. The *warm* sand was a *rough* carpet under my feet. How refreshing to feel the *cold, splashing* waves as I dashed into the water!

Now read the same story without the adjectives. Which story makes a better "word picture"?

SUMMER FUN

I have memories of my days at the shore. The sun shone on me at play. The sand was a carpet under my feet. How refreshing to feel the waves as I dashed into the water!

When we write a sentence or a story without adjectives, it is like making a picture without crayons or paints. Our picture may be very nice, but it will be much better if we add some color. Try to be an artist with words. Think of adjectives to describe the following nouns:

_____buildings	_____traffic
_____packages	_____trees
_____sky	_____puppy
_____noises	_____movies
_____music	_____books

EXERCISE 99

Each of these sentences contains one adjective. Name the adjective and tell which noun it describes.

1 Fluffy clouds floated in the sky.
2 Keith climbed the creaky stairs.
3 Jose wore a striped jacket.
4 The broken bottle lay in the gutter.
5 Tall trees gave us shade.
6 Bernie chased the spotted butterfly.
7 Loud music filled the room.
8 We played on the green hills.
9 Happy children worked together.
10 Fast trucks raced down the street.

EXERCISE 100

Copy each noun and write an adjective before it:

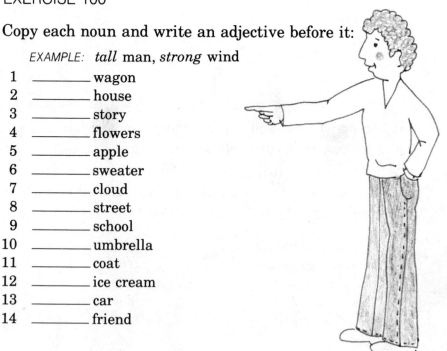

EXAMPLE: *tall* man, *strong* wind

1 _____ wagon
2 _____ house
3 _____ story
4 _____ flowers
5 _____ apple
6 _____ sweater
7 _____ cloud
8 _____ street
9 _____ school
10 _____ umbrella
11 _____ coat
12 _____ ice cream
13 _____ car
14 _____ friend

EXERCISE 101

Copy the following adjectives and write a noun which each adjective might describe:

EXAMPLE: bitter *lemon*, chilly *wind*

1 green _____
2 high _____
3 little _____
4 sweet _____
5 cold _____
6 shiny _____
7 fast _____
8 funny _____
9 hard _____
10 sad _____
11 soft _____
12 bright _____

EXERCISE 102

Each of the following sentences contains one adjective. Copy the sentences, and draw one line under the adjective and two lines under the noun it describes. To find the adjective, ask yourself the question *What kind?* before the noun.

EXAMPLE: <u>Tiny</u> <u>flowers</u> grew in the field. (*What kind* of flowers?)

1 The funny clown made us laugh.
2 The bright sun hurt my eyes.
3 Walt brought a big lunch to the picnic.
4 The police car went down the street.
5 Mr. Lopez carried the heavy ladder.
6 Our neatest work was hung in the classroom.
7 Shiny boots stood together.
8 Cheerful birds sang in the trees.
9 Keep a sharp pencil with your notebooks.
10 The playful kittens tangled the yarn.

244

EXERCISE 103

Read carefully the adjectives listed below. Find the correct adjective for each sentence, then write the sentences and underline the adjectives.

bashful	long
noisy	colorful
cold	torn
skillful	scary
ripe	fat

1 The _____ wind blew from the north.
2 _____ apples hung from the tree.
3 _____laughter came from the party.
4 The _____ face frightened the children.
5 Mrs. Pierce mended Patty's _____ dress.
6 _____ pigs ate from their trough.
7 _____ leaves fell from the tree.
8 The _____ child was afraid to speak.
9 A _____ line waited outside the movie.
10 The _____ acrobat swung from the bar.

ADJECTIVAL PHRASES

WHAT IS YELLOW?

by Mary O'Neil

Yellow is the color of the sun
The feeling of fun
The yolk of an egg
A duck's bill
A canary bird
And a daffodil . . .

We have already learned that words which describe nouns are called *adjectives*. Sometimes we use a *group of words* to describe a noun. This word group is called an *adjectival phrase*.

An adjectival phrase does the same work as an adjective; it modifies a noun. In a phrase, several words work together to answer the question *what kind*. For example, in the poem "What Is Yellow?" the poet describes what yellow means to her. She uses several adjectival phrases:

> . . . the color *of the sun*   (What kind of color?)
> . . . feeling *of fun*   (What kind of feeling?)
> . . . yolk *of an egg*   (What kind of yolk?)

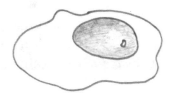

Position of Adjectives and Adjectival Phrases

Although adjectives and adjectival phrases do the same work of modifying nouns, they are usually found in different places in a sentence. An adjective usually comes *before* the noun it describes. An adjectival phrase usually comes *after* the noun it describes. Read these sets of sentences. Notice how adjectival phrases after nouns make sentences come alive.

> The *big* box fell down the steps.   (*big*—adjective)
> The big box *of groceries* fell down the steps.
>   (*of groceries*—adjectival phrase)

The *loud* sound startled the girls.   (*loud*—adjective)
The loud sound *of thunder* startled the girls *on their bikes*.
     (*of thunder*—adjectival phrase; *on their bikes*—
     adjectival phrase)

A *wooden* table stood in the corner.   (*wooden*—adjective)
A table *of highly polished wood* stood in the corner.
     (*of highly polished wood*—adjectival phrase)

In the first set of sentences, the phrase *of groceries* tells *what kind* of box. These words give a clearer picture of what happened. In the second and third sets of sentences, the following are adjectival phrases:

sound *of thunder*   (kind of sound)
girls *on their bikes*   (kind of girls)
table *of highly polished wood* (kind of table)

EXERCISE 104

Read each sentence orally. The adjectival phrase is in italics. Name the noun it describes.

1 The balloon *of water* burst suddenly.
2 The man *in the gray suit* is my uncle.
3 I dropped a bottle *of soda*.
4 The members *of the club* met in our basement.
5 The book *about Indians* was exciting.
6 The statue *of marble* shone in the sun.
7 The litter *of kittens* slept in the box.
8 The girl *with my sister* is Dawn.
9 Piles *of paper* fell from my desk.
10 The driver *of the van* slowed down.

EXERCISE 105

In the following sentences the adjectival phrase is in italics. Copy the sentences. Draw one line under the adjectival phrase and two lines under the noun it describes.

EXAMPLE: Karen fixed the vase of flowers.

1 A flock *of geese* flew across the sky.
2 The child *in the costume* said, "Trick or treat!"
3 The school bag *with the strap* is mine.
4 My father is a friend *of Mr. Davis.*
5 The driver *of the cab* stopped at the corner.
6 Lisa drew a picture *of her house.*
7 The sound *of the fan* filled the room.
8 Dan helped the lady *with the package.*
9 Flags *of many colors* passed by.
10 Bottles *of glue* lined the shelves.

EXERCISE 106

Copy these adjectival phrases. Write a noun which the adjectival phrase might describe.

1 _____ of blue wool
2 _____ with a bike
3 _____ of fruit
4 _____ of many kinds
5 _____ with large windows
6 _____ of the television
7 _____ with brown eyes
8 _____ of red plaid
9 _____ of milk
10 _____ with a kite

EXERCISE 107

Read the following sentences orally. The noun in each sentence is in italics. Find the word or group of words that describe the noun, and tell whether it is an adjective or an adjectival phrase.

1 Busy *shoppers* rushed from store to store.
2 The mailman carried a *sack* of letters.
3 *Children* with balloons ran to the bus.
4 The playful *cubs* stayed near their mother.
5 A soft *quilt* warmed the bed.
6 *Flakes* of snow fell to the ground.
7 Laura read the *recipe* for gingerbread.
8 Sharp *knives* are in the drawer.
9 Our teacher gave us new *books*.
10 *Herds* of buffalo once grazed here.
11 Small *pieces* of colored paper covered the floor.
12 Susan has a new *radio*.
13 Dark *clouds* warned us that a storm was coming.
14 The *pilot* of that airplane is my uncle.

ARTICLES—NOUN POINTERS

Adjectives and adjective phrases describe nouns. There are certain other words that tell that a noun will follow. These words are called *articles* or *determiners*. They are like the clues a detective uses in solving a mystery. These little words point out important nouns in sentences. The articles are *a, an,* and *the.*

The child held his red balloon. *(The* points out the noun *child.)*

A cloud floated across *the* sky. *(A* points out the noun *cloud.)*

(The points out the noun *sky.)*

May I have *an* apple?   *(An* points out the noun *apple.)*

A is used before a word that begins with a consonant. *An* is used before a word that begins with a vowel.

EXERCISE 108

In the following sentences the nouns are in italics. Name the article that points out each noun.

1   Each person carried a *sign*.
2   The *bell* rang loudly.
3   Watch the *movie*, please.
4   Tara found an *egg* in the *nest*.
5   Is the *lawn* mowed yet?
6   The *program* is almost finished.
7   Maura wrapped the *gift* carefully.
8   A *raccoon* came into the *yard*.
9   An *eagle* flies very high.
10 Close the *window* when you leave.

250

EXERCISE 109

Copy the following sentences. Write *a* or *an* on the line before each sentence. The first word of a sentence is written with a capital letter.

EXAMPLE: **A** snake crawled under the bush.
An Indian made this necklace.

1 _____ horse rode past our house.
2 _____ large door led into the hall.
3 _____ ape swung from branch to branch.
4 _____ snowman stood on the hill.
5 _____ icicle hung from our porch.
6 _____ opposite of happy is sad.
7 _____ funny cartoon made us laugh.
8 _____ tugboat pulled the ship into the port.
9 _____ tiny flower grew on the sidewalk.

EXERCISE 110

Copy the following sentences. Draw one line under the article or determiner, and two lines under the noun it points out.

EXAMPLE: <u>The</u> <u>cricket</u> played its summer song.

1 The man snored loudly.
2 We learned the work in school.
3 I ate an egg for breakfast.
4 May I have a glass of milk?
5 The rain beat on my window.
6 Pass the sugar, please.
7 Ronnie gave me a plant.
8 The door slammed loudly.
9 A nurse helped us at camp.
10 Would you like an orange?

Other Words That Point Out

> Sometimes words need a helper
> As much as a dog needs a bone,
> But don't confuse the weaklings
> With words that stand alone!
>
> Say *"This* chair belongs *beside me,*
> And *that* one belongs *over there."*
> *This here* and *that there* are extras,
> In our sentences they may be *no where!*

This and *that* are special words we use to point out a noun. Sometimes children add words by saying *this here* and *that there.* If we do this, we keep *this* and *that* from doing their job alone.

Everybody likes to finish a job by himself. A helper can get in the way and ruin what we are doing. Don't let extra helpers hurt your sentences!

Use the word *this* to point out things that are *near at hand.* Use the word *that* to point out things that are *at a distance.* Notice how these words are used in sentences:

> *This* work is well done.   (near at hand)
> *That* horse won the race.   (at a distance)

EXERCISE 111

Copy the following sentences. Write the word *this* or *that* in the blank space.

1 _____ ring belongs to me.   (near at hand)
2 Lincoln lived in_____ house.   (at a distance)
3 Can you see _____ picture?   (near at hand)
4 Mother gave me _____ watch.   (near at hand)

continued on next page

5 We will ask our teacher about _____ tree. (at a distance)
6 _____ farm is the largest in the state. (at a distance)
7 _____ bucket leaks. (near at hand)
8 Did you bake _____ bread? (near at hand)
9 _____ cotton grew in South Carolina. (at a distance)
10 Did your father cook _____ dinner? (near at hand)

ADVERBS

Adverbs describe or modify the verb in a sentence.

The worm looked *up*
As the robin peered *down*.
"It's just as I feared,"
He said with a frown.

"*Soon* his beak will come *in*
And I'll be pulled *out!*
Somebody save me."
He started to shout!

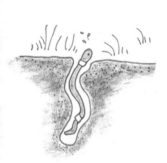

"*Today* he is *here*,
Tomorrow he'll be *back!*
No doubt, it's time *soon*
For the Mrs. to pack!"

"*Now* I'll make a new tunnel—
To where?—I'll not tell!"
All his family crawled *forward*.
He *next* waved his "Farewell"!

In this poem about the sly worm and the hungry robin, there are many little words that tell us *when* and *where* events of the story happened. For example, the words *up*, *down, in, out, here, back,* and *forward* tell us *where* something occurred. Other words, *soon, today, tomorrow, next,* and *now,* tell us *when* something happened. Words that answer to *when* and *where* in a sentence are called *adverbs.*

Adverbs, and adverb phrases, describe or *modify* the verb in a sentence. We will study two kinds of adverbs: adverbs of *time* and adverbs of *place.* These adverbs will modify or add to the meaning of *verbs.*

Adverbs of Time

An *adverb of time* answers the question *when* or *how often.* Notice the italicized adverbs in these sentences:

The bus will come *soon.*	*(Soon* tells *when* the bus will come.)
We will leave *early.*	*(Early* tells *when* we will leave.)
Let's work together *now.*	*(Now* tells *when* we will work.)
We went to the zoo *twice.*	*(Twice* tells *how often* we went to the zoo.)

The following are *adverbs of time* for you to learn and use in sentences of your own.

again	early	late	often	today
already	ever	never	once	tomorrow
always	finally	next	sometimes	twice
before	first	now	soon	yesterday

EXERCISE 112

In the sentences on page 254 find the *adverb of time.*

Remember to ask the question *when* or *how often* after the verb.

EXAMPLE: John *finally* arrived home.   *arrived* (when?)
                                        finally (adverb of time)

1   I will finish the ironing now.
2   Bill went to the store twice.
3   We often visit my grandparents.
4   Soon summer will come.
5   Paul never forgets the rules for safety.
6   Always begin each sentence with a capital letter.
7   We finally went to bed.
8   Write the sentences now.
9   He came late for class.
10   Sherry, do the problem again.

EXERCISE 113

The verb in each of the following sentences is in italics. Copy the sentences; then draw one line under the verb and two lines under the adverb of time that modifies the verb.

EXAMPLE: Please come now, Jimmy.

1   We *left* late at night.
2   Our last trip *is* tomorrow.
3   Joanne *went* to the dentist yesterday.
4   Many Indians now *live* in cities.
5   Luke *finished* early in the morning.
6   *Visit* us soon.
7   Children often *play* with balloons.
8   Tomorrow we *take* our projects to school with us.
9   Sometimes clouds *bring* rain.
10   Never *play* with matches.

EXERCISE 114

Select an adverb of time from the following list to complete each sentence:

soon often never early finally now yesterday

1 Finish the dishes _____ , Pam.
2 My birthday_____ came.
3 I visit the library_____ .
4 _____ run on the stairs.
5 The plane will leave _____ in the morning.
6 David went _____ .
7 The girls will go _____ .
8 Most farmers rise _____ .
9 _____ the painting was completed.
10 Our family_____ lives in an apartment.

Adverbs of Place

Adverbs of place answer the question *where*. The italicized words in these sentences are adverbs of place:

Let's play *outside*.	*(Outside* tells *where* we will play.)
May we come *in?*	*(In* tells *where* we may come.)
I looked *everywhere!*	*(Everywhere* tells *where* I looked.)
The baby is asleep *upstairs.*	*(Upstairs* tells *where* the baby is sleeping.)

The following are adverbs of place for you to learn and use in sentences.

above	backward	far	in	there
ahead	below	forth	inside	up
away	down	forward	out	upstairs
back	everywhere	here	outside	within

EXERCISE 115

In the following sentences, find the adverb of place. Remember to ask the question *where* after the verb.

EXAMPLE: The sky is above the earth.   *is* (where?)
above (adverb of place)

1   A black crow flew above the trees.
2   Put up your umbrella, Peggy.
3   The baseball game was played outside.
4   The soldiers marched forward.
5   Is Julian inside?
6   Pedro looked everywhere for the wrench.
7   The puppet's head shook up and down.
8   Bring your bike inside.
9   Put it there.
10   Angelo went upstairs.

EXERCISE 116

Copy the following sentences. The verb is in italics. Draw one line under the verb and two lines under the adverb of place that modifies the verb.

EXAMPLE: <u>Bring</u> the school bag <u>here</u>.

1   The old lady *stepped* down from the bus.
2   On Saturday we *worked* outside.
3   Please *come* back.
4   The parade *moved* forward.
5   That chair *belongs* there.
6   The seagulls *swooped* down.
7   The ship *sailed* forth from the port.
8   The excited children *ran* downstairs.
9   Mr. Peters *drove* back.
10   *Carry* the box inside.

EXERCISE 117

Select an adverb of place from the following list to complete each sentence:

away   everywhere   below   outside   here   far   down   up

1   Pick _____ your toys.
2   Jim put his bat _____ .
3   If it rains, we cannot play_____ .
4   Tiny pieces of paper fell _____ .
5   The next town is _____ .
6   _____ are the directions.
7   Are you going _____ for the summer?
8   The basement is _____ the first floor.
9   _____ are your skates.
10   Lie _____ , Ruff.

EXERCISE 118

Draw two columns on your paper. At the top of the first column write *Adverbs of Time*. At the top of the second column write *Adverbs of Place*. Put the following adverbs in the correct column.

early	out	today	always
down	now	below	never
next	away	again	inside
twice	up	everywhere	far

ADVERBIAL PHRASES

We have studied two kinds of adverbs: adverbs of time and adverbs of place. There are also *groups of words* which do the same work as an adverb. Read the following sentences:

The electrician will come *tomorrow*. (adverb of time—When?)

The electrician will come *in the morning*. (adverbial phrase of time—When?)

We ate our lunch *outside*. (adverb of place—Where?)

We ate our lunch *on the lawn*. (adverbial phrase of place—Where?)

Groups of words which do the same work as an adverb are called *adverbial phrases*.

EXERCISE 119

Copy these adverbial phrases. Write a verb which the adverb phrase might modify.

ADVERBIAL PHRASE OF TIME	*ADVERBIAL PHRASE OF PLACE*
1 _____ in the morning	1 _____ near the fireplace
2 _____ at noon	2 _____ to the game
3 _____ before dinner	3 _____ in the pond
4 _____ after the game	4 _____ by the kitchen door
5 _____ before school	5 _____ at home

EXERCISE 120

In the following sentences the adverbial phrase is in italics.
Write the verb which the phrase modifies on your paper.

1   *At no time* be unkind.
2   My father rises *at an early hour*.
3   We swam *in the pool*.
4   Airplanes fly *over our school*.
5   Bananas grow *on tall trees*.
6   My brother hid *under the porch*.
7   The jogger ran *down the road*.
8   A thunderstorm will come *during the afternoon*.
9   Joan went to the doctor *before school*.
10 We shall meet *after dinner*.

EXERCISE 121

Tell whether the italicized words are adverbs or adverbial
phrases:

1   They bloom *on leafy bushes*.
2   Shells are *often* found on ocean beaches.
3   The little violet has *always* been my favorite flower.
4   I am gazing *at those beautiful horses*.
5   Father went *to the garage*.
6   I will try *again*.
7   The bee flew *away*.
8   Evergreen trees will not grow *in that soil*.
9   We strolled *down the path*.
10 *Tomorrow* we are going to the amusement park.
11 It will *soon* be vacation.
12 They will leave *early*.
13 All the work was done *outside*.
14 The little children are *at the playground*.

USING WORDS CORRECTLY

"GOOD" and "WELL"

The words that we have studied so far all have special jobs to do. When we use words correctly, we strengthen our sentences.

Two words which must be used with care are *good* and *well. Good* is used to describe a person or thing. *Good* is an adjective and tells *what kind. Well* is used to modify a verb. *Well* is an adverb and tells *how something is done.* Notice the use of good and well in these sentences:

Be a *good* writer.   (Kind of writer)
You sing *well.*   (Sing how)

Remember that *good* tells *what kind* and *well* tells *how something is done.*

EXERCISE 122

Write the following sentences, filling in each blank with *good* or *well:*

1   Ellen roller-skates _____ .
2   Is Beth a _____ reader?
3   _____ food keeps us healthy.
4   Clean your room _____ , Sharon.
5   Do a _____ deed every day.
6   Wanda leads the team _____ .
7   Mom bakes _____ cakes.
8   Ken plays checkers _____ .
9   I watched a _____ movie last night.
10   Try to be a _____ sport in games.

THE "NO" WORDS

There are other words that can hurt our writing and speaking if we do not use them correctly. These are the "no" words. The words *no, not,* and *never* belong to this family. Never use two "no" words together in a sentence. Notice the "no" words in these sentences:

> Mr. Brown has *no* car.
> Rick did *not* bring his sister.
> Chris has *never* been late.

Don't be tricked by the "no" words, especially when they are used in a contraction. The "no" contractions are *doesn't, don't, hasn't, haven't, isn't, aren't,* and *weren't.* Remember that the little word *not* is in each of these words. In using these contractions, we say *any* or *ever* after them. Read these sentences:

> Joe hasn't *any* candy.
> We don't *ever* go to that lake.

The words *ever* and *never* can be tricky unless we are careful. Notice the use of *ever* and *never* in these sentences:

Trucks *never* use this street.
We don't *ever* use this street.

Never was changed to *ever* because "no" was used in the

contraction *don't*. Had we not changed *never* to *ever,* we would have had two "no" words in the same sentence.

EXERCISE 123

Copy the following sentences. Choose the correct word from the words in the parentheses.

1 I did not buy (any, no) orange juice.
2 No one in our family (ever, never) misses the concert.
3 The baby does not make (any, no) noise.
4 We did not carry (any, no) lunch to school today.
5 He has (ever, never) seen a soccer game.
6 I have (ever, never) traveled on the subway.
7 Didn't he do (any, no) work?
8 Marie didn't eat (any, no) lima beans.
9 Judy has (ever, never) seen the Grand Canyon.
10 There are not (any, no) radishes in our garden.
11 We did not think that we would (ever, never) go.
12 There were not (any, no) cookies in the jar.
13 The class had (any, no) erasers.
14 I had (any, no) money with me.

WORD STUDY

Dictionary Skills

In writing, we learn to use a *hyphen* to divide words into syllables at the end of a line. A *hyphen* is a short dash (-). It is used to separate words into syllables. Part of a word may be written at the end of one line, and the rest of the word at the beginning of the next line, by using a hyphen.

The word *Sunday* contains two syllables, *Sun* and *day*. When this word is divided, *Sun-* is written at the end of the first line, and *day* is written at the beginning of the second line.

The following words are divided into correct syllables:

speak- ing	bal- loon	gob- lin
spoon- ful	sis- ter	al- low

When you divide a word into syllables, listen for the vowel sounds in the word. A *syllable* is a part of a word that contains one vowel sound. Therefore, if a word has one vowel sound, it contains one syllable. If it has two vowel sounds, it contains two syllables. Remember, we do not *count* the number of vowels, because sometimes two vowels can make one *sound*. Words that have only one syllable, or one vowel sound, may not be divided. *Boy, care, fear,* and *sun* are words that have only one syllable.

When a word is written on two lines, place the hyphen at the end of the first line with the first part of the word, then write the rest of the word at the beginning of the next line. If you are not sure of the correct syllables, look the word up in the dictionary.

In the dictionary, words are divided into syllables. For example, when you look up the word *wagon,* you find it is written **wag•on.** This means that it can be divided only between the *g* and the *o.*   The word *broadcast* contains two syllables. Notice how it is divided in this sentence:

Susan was the announcer when her class gave a *broadcast* on travel by air.

EXERCISE 124

A   Find these words in the dictionary. Divide them into syllables.

wallet	muddy	control
trailer	escape	needle
monkey	cutout	farmer

B   Find each of these words in the dictionary. Write the words in correct syllables. Use each word in a sentence of your own.

1	juggle	4	insect	7	thirteen
2	driver	5	heater	8	stiffen
3	drown	6	igloo	9	path

Synonyms

We should not use the same words over and over when we speak or write. We should try to find words of similar meaning. Words that mean nearly the same thing are called *synonyms*. Here are four sets of words. Each group of two words are synonyms.

look—see   glad—happy   shout—yell   start—begin

Synonyms are words that have nearly the same meaning.

EXERCISE 125

The following sentences are arranged in groups. Each group contains two words with nearly the same meaning. Name these synonyms.

1 Can you see the other side of the canyon?
   Come and look at these fish.

2 I will be glad to have you come to my party.
   My Mom was happy with my test paper.

3 It is not necessary to shout.
   Did you yell for me?

4 We will begin after our lunch.
   When did the movie start?

EXERCISE 126

Copy the sentences in Exercise 125. Draw a line under each synonym.

EXERCISE 127

Copy the words in Column A. Find the correct synonym from Column B and write it next to its partner. Use these words in sentences of your own.

COLUMN A	COLUMN B
1 look	yell
2 glad	begin
3 shout	see
4 start	happy

Antonyms

Go and *come* are opposites. When our dog follows us to school, we say *"Go* home!" When we return from school, we call *"Come,* Freckles!" The words *go* and *come* are opposites. *Go* expresses motion *away from* the speaker; *come* expresses motion *toward* the speaker.

> My two brothers always *come* home early. *(Motion toward the speaker)*
>
> Father and Mother *go* to New York every year. *(Motion away from the speaker)*

Words that have opposite meanings are called *antonyms*.

EXERCISE 128

Copy the following sentences. Use *come* or *go* correctly in each blank.

1   Katie, you may _____ to Lynn's house after school.
2   I _____ to bed early every night.
3   On Friday I shall _____ to Grandmother's.
4   _____ here, Thomas.
5   When can you _____ to our house?
6   Where shall we _____ for our vacation?
7   Will you _____ to visit me?
8   Len, please _____ to the store for me.
9   We _____ swimming in the lake every summer.
10   Please _____ to see us again.
11   Let us _____ down to the beach.
12   Ask your mother if you may _____ to the show with me.

"RIGHT" and "WRONG"

We often use the antonyms *right* or *wrong*. When we say that something is *correct* or *true,* we use the word *right*. If something is *not correct,* we use the word *wrong.*

> Connie gave the *right* answer.
> You brought the *wrong* book.

EXERCISE 129

Copy these sentences. Use an antonym for the word printed in italics.

1 Your answer is *right,* Josh.
2 This is the *wrong* size.
3 Myra, you have chosen the *wrong* color.
4 Dick gave the *right* meaning for the word.
5 That is *wrong,* Laura.
6 Dorothy put the letter into the *wrong* envelope.
7 Did you speak at the *wrong* time, Al?
8 They gave the award to the *right* boy.
9 Did you give the customer the *right* change?
10 Edward dialed the *wrong* number.

Homonyms

"RIGHT" or "WRITE"

We are now familiar with the word *right,* and know what it means. This word has a homonym, *write. Write* means *to mark letters or words on paper with a pen or pencil.* See how these two homonyms are used:

Always *write* neatly.
You have the *right* answer.

Homonyms are words that sound alike, but are
not spelled alike and do not mean the same thing.

EXERCISE 130

Copy the following sentences. Fill in each blank with *write*
or *right*.

1   Where did you _____ the address?
2   Pat always does the _____ thing.
3   _____ your invitations clearly.
4   Mary, _____ your name here.
5   I will _____ a letter to my friend.
6   That is the _____ way to salute the flag.
7   I cannot _____ with this pen.
8   That is _____, Lee.
9   When you _____, be careful to form each letter correctly.
10 In the days of King Alfred, many people did not know how
    to _____ .
11 On Washington's sword are the words, "Do _____ ; fear no
    one."
12 The _____ way to our home is down this street.
13 Did your mother _____ this note?
14 Do you know the _____ way to _____ a heading?

"TWO," "TOO," and "TO"

Three more homonyms for you to learn are: *Two, too,*
and *to.*

Now we would like to start,
That's what we would like to do;
For we're the merry sailors on
Ships *To,* and *Too,* and *Two.*

The word *two* tells *how many;* it is the number 2.

There are *two* drawers in the desk. (The number 2)

The word *too* means *more than enough* or *also.*

This coat is *too* large.   (More than enough)
You may go, *too.*   (Also)

The word *to* may indicate motion toward.

They sailed away *to* a far-off land.   (Motion toward)

The word *to* may also be used before words such as *come,*
speak, sing, and *play.*

It is your turn *to* speak.   (Used before *speak*)

EXERCISE 131

Copy the following sentences. Use *to, too,* or *two* in the
blanks in each sentence.

1   May I go _____ ?
2   I saw _____ hawks in the sky.
3   Teach me _____ sing.
4   It is _____ warm in the house.
5   William Penn came _____ America from England.

continued on next page

6 My little brother is _____ years old.
7 This rope is _____ long.
8 My sister caught _____ fish.
9 I asked Mother _____ come with us.
10 The cocoa is _____ hot.
11 Jerry raced me _____ the corner.
12 It rained _____ often on our vacation.
13 Would you like _____ see the ocean?
14 I like candy _____ .

Contractions

We have learned that contractions are words formed by joining two words together. When we write contractions, we leave out some letter or letters and put an apostrophe in place of them.

"DOESN'T" and "DON'T"

Doesn't and *don't* are two contractions you will learn this year. *Doesn't* is the contraction for *does not*. When these two words are joined together, the *o* in *not* is left out and an apostrophe takes its place. *Don't* is the contraction for *do not*. When these words are joined, the *o* in *not* is left out and an apostrophe takes its place.

> He *doesn't* look like a football player.
> They *don't* know the rules of the game.

WORDS	CONTRACTIONS	CHANGES
does not	doesn't	Take the *o* out. Put the apostrophe (') in.
do not	don't	Take the *o* out. Put the apostrophe (') in.

EXERCISE 132

Copy the following sentences. Use contractions for the words *do not* and *does not*.

1 These marbles do not belong to James.
2 The roads do not seem crowded.
3 Mother does not often wear her fur coat.
4 I do not see the deer.
5 Careless people do not obey traffic rules.
6 That problem does not seem difficult to me.
7 Periods do not follow interrogative sentences.
8 Coffee does not grow in the United States.
9 My brother does not go to early class every day.
10 You and your sister do not look alike.

The contraction *doesn't* should be used in speaking of one person, one place, or one thing.

> This book *doesn't* belong to me.   (One thing)

The word *don't* should be used in speaking of more than one person, place, or thing. *Don't* is used with the pronouns *you* and *I*.

> They *don't* speak English.   (More than one person)
> I *don't* like to be late.   (With the word *I*)
> *Don't* you know where we live?   (With the word *you*)

EXERCISE 133

Copy the following sentences. Select the correct word from the words in each parentheses.

1 My sister (doesn't, don't) like liver.
2 These gloves (doesn't, don't) fit me.

continued on next page

3   (Doesn't, don't) you like snowstorms?

4   I (doesn't, don't) play ball very well.

5   Mary (doesn't, don't) live on my street.

6   The twins (doesn't, don't) drink tea or coffee.

7   Father (doesn't, don't) eat fried meat.

8   I (doesn't don't) think you should go today.

9   My sister (doesn't, don't) play the piano.

10 (Doesn't, don't) the sun set in the west?

11 We (doesn't, don't) leave our toys on the floor.

12 Why (doesn't, don't) you bring your basketball?

13 John (doesn't, don't) understand your directions.

14 I (doesn't, don't) often go downtown.

15 My parents (doesn't, don't) allow me to go there alone.

EXERCISE 134   [Chapter Challenge]

Read the following paragraph. On a separate paper, fill in the blanks for a self-check on what you have learned in this chapter.

SURPRISES

[1]Our backyard is full of delightful surprises for me. [2]The pleasures come while I play there each season. [3]In the spring, I pick yellow flowers. [4]My friends and I often swim in our pool in the summer. [5]In the fall, I like to gather the bright, colorful leaves that decorate the trees. [6]But best of all, I enjoy the blanket of snow that covers the whole yard in the winter. [7]Don't you agree that the surprises that come and go with the seasons make our backyard a happy place?

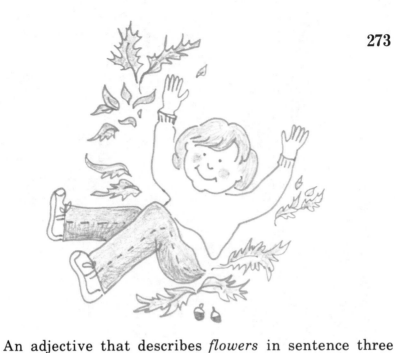

1 An adjective that describes *flowers* in sentence three is _____.

2 An article that points out the noun *summer* in sentence four is _____.

3 An adverb of place that modifies *play* in sentence two is _____.

4 An adverb of time that modifies *swim* in sentence four is _____.

5 The adjective that describes *surprises* in sentence one is _____.

6 The adjectival phrase that describes *blanket* in sentence six is _____.

7 Adjectives that describe *leaves* in sentence five are _____ and _____.

8 A word that means the same as *happy* in sentence seven is _____.

9 The contraction for *do not* is found in the last sentence. It is _____.

10 The two words that mean the opposite of each other in sentence seven are _____ and _____.

CHAPTER FIVE

Capitalization and Punctuation

Have you ever watched a parade? If you have, you probably noticed many interesting things. Who led the parade? How were the marchers dressed? Did anybody have a special job to do?

Let us use our imaginations for a moment. Pretend you are again watching a most exciting parade. Close your eyes. Now change all the paraders. Change their bright, high hats into ordinary hats; their marching uniforms into plain, gray jackets. Take away the special parts—no floats, no baton twirlers, no clowns, no drill teams. Everybody now looks the same. Can you see them marching together row after row? Let us leave the music out. Just listen to the steady march, march, march of their feet. All the people look just alike, are dressed in a dull color, and are not doing anything but marching in silence.

Which parade would you like better? Do you like a parade with special people doing exciting things and wearing colorful uniforms? Would you rather watch the kind of parade we just imagined? Most of you would choose the first parade. Why? It would be more interesting and more exciting!

CAPITALIZATION

Whenever we write or speak, the results should resemble a colorful parade. Our sentences should be so interesting that people will enjoy reading them. Sometimes our sentences can be very boring. This happens when we do not use all the special marks of punctuation and capital letters needed. A capital letter is like the leader of the band. Let us review the use of capital letters.

Capital Letters Begin Sentences

A capital letter is really a word leader. It begins a sentence. We have learned the four kinds of sentences: declarative, interrogative, exclamatory, and imperative. These sentences are like four special marching teams in a parade. The first word of a sentence begins with a capital letter. Look at these four sentences:

The parade will start on
   Cottman Avenue.   (Declarative)
When will the parade start?   (Interrogative)
Oh, how I love a parade!   (Exclamatory)
Begin the music now.   (Imperative)

These four kinds of sentences have different punctuation marks to complete them, and all the sentences begin with capital letters.

> **Remember:**
> *The first word of every sentence begins with a*
> *capital letter.*

EXERCISE 135

Copy the following sentences. Begin the first word of each
sentence with a capital letter.

1   alligators and crocodiles belong to the reptile family.
2   have you caught a fish?
3   on our vacation we visited a logging camp.
4   actions speak louder than words.
5   we have eaten all the popcorn.
6   utah was settled by Mormons.
7   tom is playing in the band.
8   the Lincoln Park Zoo is in Chicago.
9   yes, you may frost the cake.
10 my sister had her appendix removed.
11 do you play a harmonica?
12 did Alice order a hamburger?
13 wait patiently in line.
14 does a cellist work in an orchestra?

Capital Letters for Names

Read the following lines. Notice how many nouns are used
in them.

The drum majorette was *Karen*,
The drill team captain was *Tony*.
Young *Dave* dressed up in a costume
And walked with *Luke*, his pony.

Jim led the marchers with music,
Mr. Melvin directed the band.
Officer Edwards stood by to guard them;
He stopped cars by waving his hand.

Who were the people in the parade? *Karen, Tony, Dave, Jim, Mr. Melvin,* and *Officer Edwards* were there. Even *Luke*, the pet pony, was prancing along! Did you notice that each name was written with a capital letter? Whenever we write the name of a particular person, or the name of a pet, we use a capital letter.

Notice the capital letters in these sentences:

*V*ince threw the pass to *P*aul.	(Persons)
*E*llen and *K*athleen worked together.	(Persons)
I have to feed *S*nowball now.	(Pet)
My horse, *D*usty, likes to eat sugar.	(Pet)

Remember:
  The name of a particular person or pet begins with a capital letter.

EXERCISE 136

Copy the following sentences. Use capital letters wherever they are needed.

1   tiger, our cat, climbed the tree.
2   george washington was a great man.
3   my best friends are joanne and eileen.
4   ron shared his lunch with billy.
5   show albert where to put his books.
6   the magic lamp belonged to aladdin.
7   susan sent an invitation to mary alice.
8   let us walk to the corner with charles.
9   mother sent a note to penny.
10 we invited francis and margaret to play with us.
11 little kathy learned to walk by herself.
12 my snake, slither, was lost in the garden.
13 I keep petey in a cage.
14 lucy has a gerbil named crackles.

Capital Letters for Special Names

There are two classes of nouns, *common nouns* and *proper nouns*.

Remember, nouns are words that name a person, place, or thing. The words *clown, zoo,* and *balloon* are all nouns. Some nouns name a *particular* person, place, or thing. These are called *proper nouns*. Each time you write a proper noun, you begin it with a capital letter. Notice how these sentences change when we turn a common noun into a proper noun:

The *clown* carried a flowered umbrella.	(Common noun)
Bozo carried a flowered umbrella.	(Proper noun)
The music sounded on our *street*.	(Common noun)
The music sounded on *Spring Street*.	(Proper noun)

The parade will be held some *day*
   next week.   (Common noun)
The parade will be held on *Memorial Day*.   (Proper noun)

We will practice writing a proper noun with a capital letter. These proper nouns name special cities, states, countries, and schools. Notice the capital letters in these sentences:

There is a wonderful zoo in *San Diego*.   (Name of a city)
We visited my aunt in *California*.   (Name of a state)
My friend's family lived in *Japan*.   (Name of a country)
The children from *Park School* marched
   in the parade.   (Name of a school)

> **Remember:**
> *The particular names of cities, states, countries, and schools are always written with capital letters.*

EXERCISE 137

Read the following sentences. Name the proper nouns.

1 New York City is an important port.
2 Phoenix is in Arizona.
3 The children at Hudson School had a fair.
4 Many people in Germany work in factories.
5 My uncle lives in New Mexico.
6 Porter High School is very large.
7 The capital of Illinois is Springfield.
8 Alaska is our largest state.
9 Robert comes from California.
10 Kangaroos live in Australia.

ALASKA

EXERCISE 138

Copy the sentences from Exercise 137. Draw a line under the proper nouns that name a special city, state, country, or school.

EXERCISE 139

Copy the following sentences. Draw a circle around the words that should begin with a capital letter.

1 Beautiful flowers grow in hawaii.
2 florida is the Sunshine State.
3 My brother attends colby college.
4 Many people from spain now live in our country.
5 We saw the Golden Gate Bridge in san francisco.
6 kelly school is near my home.
7 There are many farms in minnesota.
8 Is new york city our largest city?

Capital Letters for Special Days

There is another time we use a capital letter—in writing names of special days. When we write the name of a holiday, like Thanksgiving, we use a capital letter.

Here are the names of holidays you should know. Each of them is always written with a capital letter.

New Year's Day	Independence Day
Arbor Day	Labor Day
Washington's Birthday	Columbus Day
Mother's Day	Halloween
Memorial Day	Thanksgiving Day
Father's Day	Flag Day
Dominion Day	Christmas

> **Remember:**
> *Names of holidays begin with capital letters.*

EXERCISE 140

Copy the following sentences. Use capital letters where they are needed.

1 We celebrate flag day in the month of June.
2 The second Sunday in May is mother's day.
3 We have turkey on thanksgiving day.
4 The first day of the year is called new year's day.
5 Most children enjoy halloween.
6 We visit the cemetery on memorial day.
7 On washington's birthday the first president of the United States is honored.
8 In July we celebrate independence day.
9 Who is honored on columbus day?
10 The Parker family had a picnic at the beach on labor day.
11 Every day should be mother's day.
12 dominion day is a Canadian holiday.
13 On arbor day we planted a tree in our yard.
14 Everybody enjoys christmas.

Capital Letters for Months and Days

The names of the days of the week and the months of the year are also special. They always begin with capital letters. Notice the capital letters in these sentences:

My birthday will be in November.
On Thursday we are going to the science museum.
We will visit our uncle on the first Sunday in March.

Do you know the names of the months of the year? They
are:

January	May	September
February	June	October
March	July	November
April	August	December

There are seven days in a week. They are:

Sunday	Wednesday	Friday
Monday	Thursday	Saturday
Tuesday		

Remember:
*The names of the days of the week or the
months of the year are always written with
capital letters.*

EXERCISE 141

Copy the following sentences. Write the name of the correct
month or day in each blank space.

1 The last month of the year is _____ .
2 We begin school in _____ .
3 The first Monday in _____ is Labor Day.
4 We celebrate Independence Day in _____ .
5 We do not go to school on _____ or on _____ .
6 Thanksgiving is always celebrated on a _____ .
7 Valentine's Day comes in _____ .
8 On the calendar, _____ is the first day of the week.
9 The twelfth of _____ is Columbus Day.
10 _____ first is called New Year's Day.

Capital Letters in Poetry

Let's jump rope! See if you can find all the words beginning with a capital letter in the following poem:

ROPE RHYME

by Eloise Greenfield

Get set, ready now, jump right in;
Bounce and kick and giggle and spin.
Listen to the rope when it hits the ground;
Listen to that clappedy-slappedy sound.
Jump right up when it tells you to;
Come back down, whatever you do.
Count to a hundred, count by ten;
Start to count all over again.
That's what jumping is all about;
Get set, ready now,
       jump
          right
             out!

Did you find all the words beginning with capital letters? In writing a poem, the first word of each line usually begins with a capital letter.

Remember:
The first word of each new line of poetry begins with a capital letter.

EXERCISE 142

Copy the following verses. Use capital letters to begin the first word in each new line.

1   every day is a fresh beginning—
every morn is the world made new.

2   sea shell, sea shell,
sing me a song, O please!
a song of ships and sailor men,
and parrots, and tropical trees.

3   kind hearts are the gardens,
kind thoughts are the roots,
kind words are the blossoms,
kind deeds are the fruits.

Capital Letters in Titles

We have learned that every new line of poetry begins with a capital letter. Capital letters are also used when we write the title of a book, poem, or story. The following titles could fit our poem about jumping rope:

"Jump Right In!"
"Clappedy-Slappedy"
"Jumping Fever"

Notice that a capital letter is used for each word in the title. We follow this rule whenever we write the title of a book or story. Here are some examples:

Make Way for Ducklings
The Wizard of Oz
Ramona the Pest

Notice that in these titles the words *for* and *of* are not capitalized. The word *the* is capitalized when it is the *first word* in the title, but not when it appears in the middle of the title. Usually, small words like *in, to, and, an, a, about, on, from, with, for,* and *by* are not written with capital letters within a title.

When we write titles, we want our readers to know whether they are titles of a poem or a book. We do this by punctuating them correctly. We use quotation marks for the titles of poems. We draw a line under the title of a book. Notice these different marks of punctuation in the following examples:

"My Donkey"   (Poem—quotation marks)
"The Purple Cow"   (Poem—quotation marks)
Eddie's Valuable Property   (Book—underlined)
How to Make Flibbers   (Book—underlined)

In a printed book, a different kind of type is used for titles of books. It is called *italics*. For example, Ursula Nordstrom wrote a book called *The Secret Language* (italics). If you were writing this title, you could not use italics. Instead, you would *underline* each word of the title.

Ursula Nordstrom wrote The Secret Language (underlined).

Remember:
Use quotation marks for the title of a poem and draw a line under the title of a book.

EXERCISE 143

Copy the titles of the following poems and books. Use capital letters where they are needed.

1   the little house on the prairie
2   goldilocks and the three bears
3   "the brown thrush"
4   the red balloon
5   pippi longstocking
6   "the children's hour"
7   "the duel"
8   first book of swimming
9   whistle for willie
10 the spooky thing

Capital Letters in Abbreviations

In our poem about people in the parade, we found the name *Mr. Melvin.* There are two ways we can write this name—*Mister Melvin,* or *Mr. Melvin.* Mr. is an *abbreviation* for Mister. An abbreviation is *the short form of writing a word.* We must remember certain rules in using abbreviations.

Some abbreviations begin with a capital letter, and some are not capitalized. You must ask first, "What is the word that I intend to shorten or abbreviate?" In writing the abbreviation for words like *inch* or *pint,* the abbreviation does not begin with a capital letter, because the word itself does not begin with a capital letter. When you abbreviate a word like *Doctor, Mister, January,* or *Monday,* you use a capital letter, because each word begins with a capital letter. As we learned in Chapter Five, each state is now abbreviated by

288

two capital letters; for example, California becomes CA and Florida becomes FL.

Some abbreviations are followed by a period, and some are not. *Most* abbreviations take a period, except for the new abbreviations for state names and symbols of the metric system.

We should not use too many abbreviations in our own writing. Some that you should become familiar with are:

TITLES

		DAYS OF THE WEEK			
Mister	Mr.	Sunday	Sun.	Thursday	Thurs.
Mistress	Mrs.	Monday	Mon.	Friday	Fri.
Doctor	Dr.	Tuesday	Tues.	Saturday	Sat.
Junior	Jr.	Wednesday	Wed.		

MONTHS		*MEASUREMENTS*		*SOME STATES*	
January	Jan.	pint	pt.	Virginia	VA
February	Feb.	gallon	gal.	Pennsylvania	PA
March	Mar.	inch	in.		
April	Apr.	foot	ft.	*ADDRESSES*	
August	Aug.	meter	m	Street	St.
September	Sept.	centi-	cm	Avenue	Ave.
October	Oct.	meter		Boulevard	Blvd.
November	Nov.	liter	l		
December	Dec.				

May, June, and July are not usually abbreviated.

> **Remember:**
> *1 An abbreviation is the short form of writing a word.*
> *2 Most abbreviations are followed by a period.*
> *3 An abbreviation begins with a capital letter if the word itself begins with a capital letter.*

EXERCISE 144

Copy the words from Column A. Write the correct abbreviation from Column B next to each word in Column A.

COLUMN A		COLUMN B
____ 1	Pennsylvania	Fri.
____ 2	Doctor	Jr.
____ 3	Friday	cm
____ 4	November	PA
____ 5	centimeter	Aug.
____ 6	Mister	Dr.
____ 7	August	Mon.
____ 8	gallon	gal.
____ 9	Monday	Mr.
____ 10	Junior	Nov.

EXERCISE 145

Copy the following sentences. Place a period after each abbreviation.

1 The abbreviation for Saturday is Sat
2 Mon is the short way of writing Monday.
3 Mrs William Scully is Marcella's aunt.
4 John wrote a letter to Dr Joseph Kilroy.

continued on next page

5   The short form of the word gallon is gal
6   My uncle's address is sometimes written 2235 St Louis Ave
7   The word pint is written pt on our milk bill.
8   The short form of Friday is Fri
9   Oct is the abbreviation for October.
10 The advertisement said that the contest would be held on Feb 16.

EXERCISE 146

Copy the following sentences. Write the correct abbreviation in each blank. Use capital letters and periods where they are needed.

1   Pennsylvania is sometimes written _____ .
2   _____ is the abbreviation for street.
3   The word pint was written _____ on Mother's shopping list.
4   We may sometimes see Avenue written as _____ .
5   _____ is the short way of writing Tuesday.
6   Father sent me to _____ Swanson's office.
7   My grandmother's name is _____ Anthony Blair.
8   The abbreviation for the state of Virginia is _____ .
9   _____ Joseph Fox removed my tonsils.
10 The short form for inch is _____ .

Capital Letters for Initials and "I"

We have learned that an abbreviation is the short form of writing a word. An abbreviation is usually followed by a period. If the word itself begins with a capital letter, then the abbreviation also begins with a capital letter.

Read the following sentences. Notice the names of the people mentioned:

Fred P. Jones set up benches.
Peter M. King is our mayor.
L. M. Smith and I judged the contest.
Mary A. Burke wrote this story.

Some of these names have been shortened to just a capital letter. This letter is called an *initial*. We often use initials instead of writing our name in full.

The people named are Fred P. Jones, Peter M. King, L. M. Smith, and Mary A. Burke. Can you imagine what Fred's middle name might be? It must begin with a *P*, since this is the initial he uses. Peter's middle name begins with *M* and Mary's begins with *A*. L. M. Smith uses two initials, so we are not sure of his or her first or middle name.

There are two things to remember in writing initials. Initials are always *capital letters* and are always followed by a *period*. Notice the initials used in these sentences:

My father's name is Bernard L. Peterson.
John F. Kennedy was a great president.
I read a book written by C. S. Lewis.

There is another capital letter used in the last sentence. The letter *I* is a word when used by itself. *I* is a *pronoun* which refers to the person who is speaking. When we write the pronoun *I*, it is always capitalized. The word *I* is written correctly in each of these sentences:

I ride my bike after school
My brother and *I* jogged together.
I will come with you.

> **Remember:**
> 1 *Initials are written with capital letters and followed by a period.*
> 2 *The pronoun* **I** *is written with a capital letter.*

EXERCISE 147

Read the following sentences. Tell why the capital letters are used.

1 I have read *Charlotte's Web* by E. B. White.
2 Shall I sit with you on the train?
3 My brother is Jack L. Harris.
4 Dr. P. J. Martin took care of me.
5 Kevin T. Ford lives in New York.
6 Mr. R. S. Martinez is my neighbor.
7 I hope that I will see you again.
8 Is A. C. Hughes the mayor of your city?
9 Lisa M. Strong will be class president.
10 Louis K. Adams will finish the job.

EXERCISE 148

Copy the following sentences. Use capital letters and periods where needed.

1 john p miller is my uncle.
2 may i go with you?
3 our principal, alice k johnson, stood up.
4 a a milne wrote *winnie-the-pooh*.
5 may i try your unicycle?
6 b r jones will take you in his truck.
7 p t barnum started a circus.
8 ronald wrote his name r w casey.
9 do you think i can do it?
10 i wanted to finish first.

END PUNCTUATION

Now that we have learned where to use capital letters, let us study other special marks that will make our writing correct and clearly understood. Certain marks of punctuation are used to separate words and sentences into complete thoughts.

You have already learned how to punctuate the four kinds of sentences. A punctuation mark is placed at the end of a sentence. Read these sentences. Do you remember the reason for using each end mark?

The music began early in the morning.
May we watch the marchers?
Do not get too close to the animals.
How colorful the street looks!

There are four kinds of sentences, and each has a special mark at the end of it. Let us review the rules we have already learned:

A sentence that states a fact is called a *declarative sentence*. A *period* is placed at the end of it. These are declarative sentences:

Skillful people climbed the high mountains.
The dolphins swam beside the ship.

An *interrogative sentence* is a sentence that asks a question. We put a *question mark* (?) at the end of it. Some words used to begin interrogative sentences are *Who, When, Where, Why, How, Is, Are, Have, Has, Do,* and *Did.* These are interrogative sentences:

> Do you like ice cream and cake?
> Where will the party be?

A sentence that expresses strong feeling or emotion is called an *exclamatory sentence.* It is followed by an *exclamation point* (!). These are exclamatory sentences:

> Oh, my knee hurts!
> What fun we had on Uncle Dave's boat!

A sentence that gives a command is called an *imperative sentence.* An imperative sentence is followed by a *period.* These are imperative sentences:

> Put the bench on the sidewalk.
> Pass the papers, please.

Remember:
Every sentence is followed by a mark of punctuation.

EXERCISE 149

Read the following sentences. Tell whether each sentence is declarative, interrogative, exclamatory, or imperative.

1   Phil, do the work on the board.
2   Trucks rumbled down the street.
3   The smell of lilacs filled the room.
4   Watch out!
5   May I borrow the tape?
6   When does Mother come home from work?
7   Clean up your room.
8   There are thirty children in our class.
9   Sharon lives in Kansas City.
10   My hobby is collecting coins.
11   How well our team played!
12   Where will you go this summer?

EXERCISE 150

Copy the following sentences. Write the proper letter on the line before each sentence: *D* for declarative, *I* for interrogative, *IMP* for imperative, and *E* for exclamatory.

1   _____   Look at the sky.
2   _____   How cold the water is!
3   _____   Our class will visit the planetarium.
4   _____   The farmer grew much wheat.
5   _____   Can you stay for a while?
6   _____   Finish quickly, please.
7   _____   Wild animals roam the jungle.
8   _____   Why did David go there?
9   _____   Be careful!
10   _____   The parrot talked to the boy.

EXERCISE 151

Copy the following sentences. Put the correct punctuation mark after each sentence.

1 Is Bobby with you
2 I will meet Rona at the park
3 Pick up the papers
4 Are you Floyd's brother
5 The pizza is ready
6 How noisy the jets are
7 She brought out a pitcher of pink lemonade
8 Where is your skateboard
9 Vacation will begin soon
10 Turn out the lights

DIRECT QUOTATIONS

When we repeat the exact words that someone has spoken, we have a *direct quotation*. Listen to what some people said as they watched the parade.

> "I like the floats best," said Paula.
> Mom said, "The parade will start soon."
> The leader called, "Line up!"

Use of Quotation Marks

We use *quotation marks* (" ") to enclose a person's exact words. Quotation marks are always used in pairs. Be sure to place quotation marks at the beginning and at the end of each *direct quotation*.

Some clues that will help you recognize a direct quotation are: *said, answered, replied, asked, inquired, announced, cried, shouted, whispered,* and *repeated.* These words help us to understand how the speaker sounded. Notice how they can improve a sentence:

> Steve shouted, "I will go with you."
> Steve whispered, "I will go with you."
> Steve replied, "I will go with you."

Remember:
Quotation marks are used before and after the exact words spoken by someone.

EXERCISE 152

Copy the following sentences. Put quotation marks before and after the exact words of the speaker.

1 The man said, Watch the car for me.
2 Wanda said, It looks like rain.
3 Jim said, I like the game of checkers.
4 Little Red Riding Hood cried, What big eyes you have!
5 Robert Bruce announced, I will try again.
6 Dad said, Be good children while I am away.
7 Let's ride the ponies! shouted Tom.
8 Texas is a very large state, said Miss James.
9 Please open the window, said Mona.
10 We will invite the Indians to the Thanksgiving feast, said the Pilgrims.
11 William Penn treated the Indians kindly, said Jo.
12 I wish I could attend the party, cried Cinderella.
13 You may go if you do as I tell you, answered the fairy god-mother.
14 Help me with this, said the lady to the boys.

The Comma in Direct Quotations

We have learned to use quotation marks before and after the exact words of a speaker. Another punctuation mark often used with direct quotations is the *comma* (,). The comma is used to separate the words of the speaker from the rest of the sentence.

When the speaker's words come at the end of the sentence, we place a comma *before* the quotation:

> The cab driver said, "Your fare is six dollars."

When the speaker's words are the first words of the sentence, we put the comma *after* the last word spoken:

> "My sister is in the band," said Pat.

EXERCISE 153

Copy the following sentences. Place commas where they are needed.

1   Randy said "I'll come later."
2   Mom called "It's time for school."
3   The baby bear cried "Somebody has been sleeping in my bed."
4   "Someone has eaten my porridge" cried the other bear.
5   "There will be snow tomorrow" the weatherman announced.
6   "Let's play ball" said Joe.
7   The innkeeper said "There is no room."
8   "We are to clean the attic" said Anna.
9   The coach said "Watch what I do."
10   "Thank you, Mom" answered Tony.

Other Marks Used with Direct Quotations

Sometimes a speaker asks a question. In this case, the question mark takes the place of a comma.

"Who is in that costume?" asked Rosa.

Sometimes a speaker expresses strong feeling or emotion. Then an exclamation point is placed after his words and no comma is needed.

"How I love the waves!" shouted Ed.

> **Remember:**
> *A comma is used to set off a short direct quotation, unless a question mark or an exclamation point is needed.*

EXERCISE 154

Copy the following sentences. Place question marks or exclamation points where needed.

1 "Have you played in the sun today" asked Dad.
2 "Have you ever been in an airplane" asked Rose.
3 "Who won" shouted the happy girls.
4 "How many centimeters are in a meter" asked Paul.
5 "From what is paper made" asked Candy.
6 "Have you solved the problem" the teacher asked.
7 "Where is your bike" asked Susan.
8 "Did George win the game" questioned Larry.
9 "How is coal mined" asked Mr. Lynn.
10 "How you frightened me" exclaimed Aunt Mary.
11 "What a great time we had" exclaimed Jane.
12 "Have you finished your homework" asked Mom.

Capital Letters in Direct Quotations

Did you notice that the first word in each direct quotation began with a capital letter? Notice the use of capital letters in these sentences which contain the exact words of a speaker:

The captain said, "We're counting on you, Dick"

"Let's go now!" yelled the cheerleaders.

Remember these three things about writing direct quotations:

1 Quotation marks are placed before and after the exact words of a speaker.

2 A comma usually separates the words of the speaker from the rest of the sentence. Sometimes a question mark or an exclamation point is used instead of a comma.

3 The first word of a direct quotation begins with a capital letter.

EXERCISE 155

Correct the following sentences by using quotation marks, commas or question marks, and capital letters:

1 who was Squanto asked Mrs. Porter.
2 this is an interesting paragraph said Laura.
3 have you finished oiling your bike asked Ted.
4 Ken answered I'm finished now.
5 isn't Nashville the capital of tennessee inquired Mr. Connors.
6 may we go to the ice show asked Judy and Tim.
7 it is cool today remarked the man.
8 growing things need water explained the gardener.
9 what are clouds asked the teacher.
10 may I visit Mr. withers asked Charles.
11 Jose said I'll see you soon.
12 who was the second president asked Justin.
13 Quebec is the oldest province in canada replied the boy.
14 Where did the Pilgrims land asked Pauline.

COMMA IN DIRECT ADDRESS

At the parade, Rita met many of her classmates. She was excited to see them. These sentences tell how Rita greeted her friends:

> I'm happy to see you, *Rosa*.
> *Bobby,* did you come with John?
> *Pedro,* don't miss the tigers!
> I'm glad, *Tom,* that you're in town.

Rita called each of her friends by name. We call this *direct address,* meaning that we speak directly to a person. *Com-*

mas are used to separate the name of the person addressed from the rest of the sentence.

If the name of the person addressed is the *first* word in the sentence. the comma is placed *after* his name.

Andy, write the sentence on the chalkboard.

If the name of the person addressed is the *last* word in the sentence, the comma is placed *before* the name.

Will you play with us, Isabel?

If the name of the person addressed is in *the middle* of the sentence, a comma is placed *before and after* the name.

Please, Mrs. English, tell us a story.

Remember:
Commas are used to separate words of direct address from the rest of the sentence.

EXERCISE 156

In the following sentences, place commas to separate the words used in direct address.

1 Mr. Cobb please help us.
2 I may go Maureen if I return early.
3 Apollo stop barking at our visitor.
4 Marie I hope you will be well soon.
5 A period Cathy is placed at the end of a telling sentence.
6 James where do we obtain wool?
7 Fred we'll meet after school.
8 Have you ever visited a dairy farm Tom?
9 May I help you Mom?
10 Where does cotton grow Sam?
11 Red and yellow makes orange Willie.
12 Did you help build the snowman Jeff?

WORD STUDY

Dictionary Skills

We use a dictionary to find the *meaning* of a word. Each entry word in a dictionary is followed by one or more definitions of a word.

> **drummer** (drum′ mer)　person who plays a drum. *noun*

Sometimes a word has several definitions, as in the sample below:

> **gold** (gold).　1. a heavy, bright-yellow precious metal. Gold is used in making coins, watches, and rings.　2. made of this metal: a gold watch.　3. money in large sums; wealth; riches.　4. bright yellow.　1, 3 *noun* 2, 4 *adjective*

> *Scott, Foresman Beginning Dictionary*

EXERCISE 157

Look at the above entry for *gold*. Which definitions match the meaning of the word *gold* in the following sentences? Write the sentences, then write the number of the correct definition after each sentence.

1 *Gold* is mined in South Africa. ____
2 The man has several *gold* coins. ____
3 The queen was wearing a beautiful *gold* necklace. ____
4 *Gold* material was purchased for the banner. ____
5 The king enjoyed his *gold*. ____
6 My father's *gold* watch was stolen. ____
7 Gold is a precious metal. ____
8 She received a gold ring for her birthday. ____

EXERCISE 158

Look up the definitions of the following words in the dictionary. On a piece of paper, draw two columns. At the top of the first column, write the words *One Meaning,* and at the top of the second column put the words *More Than One Meaning.* Then write each of the words below in the proper column.

bandit	earache	outdoor	nest
test	school	guard	pin
check	herd	radish	steak

Synonyms

Synonyms are words of nearly the same meaning. To use synonyms correctly, we should consult the dictionary. Here we will find the *exact* meanings of words.

Check your dictionary for the exact meanings of these synonyms:

quick—fast   end—stop   road—path   late—tardy

EXERCISE 159

Fill in the blanks with synonyms from the above list:

1 Shovel a _____ through the snow.
2 You will be paid at the _____ of the month.
3 Ice hockey is a _____ game.
4 It was very _____ when they arrived.
5 The police officer will _____ the traffic.
6 The stalled car blocked the _____ .
7 Come early to school. Teachers do not like students to be _____ .
8 His _____ movement frightened the dog.

EXERCISE 160

The words *pleasing, enjoyable, fine,* and *attractive* have almost the same meaning as the word *nice*. The following paragraph repeats the word *nice* several times. Improve the paragraph by using synonyms for *nice*.

Mr Brady is a very *nice* bus driver. When we board the bus for school, he greets us with a *nice* smile. He is always on time and never keeps us waiting. Riding with Mr. Brady is a *nice* experience.

Antonyms

"YOUNG" and "OLD"

The books in the Book Corner were written for *young* persons. Older persons enjoy different kinds of books. *Young* and *old* are antonyms. *Young* means having to do with youth, or early life. *Old* means having lived a long time, or aged.

The *young* child carried a basket.
The *old* man walked with a cane.

EXERCISE 161

Copy the following sentences. Change the word in italics to an antonym.

1 Be kind to the *old*.
2 The *young* nurse watched the playful baby.
3 Heidi is a very *young* dog.
4 The woman who owns that house is *young*.
5 That horse is very *old*.
6 The man who played the violin was *young*.
7 The actor looked *old*.
8 The *young* man's name is Paul.
9 The *old* dog was faithful to his master.
10 We heard the *old* sailor's exciting stories.

"NEAR" and "FAR"

There are many beautiful things in this world—silvery waterfalls, lofty mountains, dark forests, and grassy plains. Some of these are *far* from our home, but there are always interesting things *near* us.

The words *near* and *far* are antonyms. Things that are *near* are close by; things that are *far* are at a distance. See how these words are used in sentences:

The lifeguard stood *near* the water.   (close by)
China is *far* from the United States.   (at a distance)

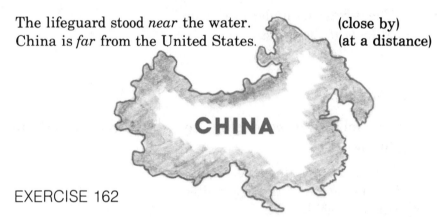

CHINA

EXERCISE 162

Copy the following sentences. Write the correct word, *near* or *far,* in the blank space.

1 Our school is _____ a playground.
2 The sun is _____ from earth.
3 _____ in the distance we see the peaks of majestic mountains.
4 Children should not play_____ from home.
5 _____ the house was a small garden.
6 _____ the grave of the Unknown Soldier stood a guard.
7 Our cottage is _____ the lake.
8 Many dairies are located _____ large cities.
9 Australia is a _____ country.
10 People came from _____ and _____ to see the parade.

Homonyms

"BEET" and "BEAT"

Beet and *beat* are two words that sound alike, but are not spelled alike and do not mean the same thing. These words are *homonyms*. *Beet* is spelled with two *e's,* and is a vegetable. The word *beat* means to strike again and again.

The *beet* grows under the ground.
Mike *beat* the drum.

EXERCISE 163

Copy the following sentences. Use *beat* or *beet* correctly in each blank space.

1   The _____ is my favorite vegetable.
2   My mother _____ the egg whites.
3   This is a pickled _____ .
4   My little brother likes to _____ his drum.
5   The heart should _____ firmly.
6   Where is the _____ field?
7   Paul _____ the rug for his mother.
8   The cruel man _____ his horse.
9   Did you ever see a white _____ ?
10   All afternoon the rain _____ against the window.

"CENT" and "SENT"

Susan said, "Our class sent thank-you letters to the chaperones of our class trip." The word *sent* is a *homonym* for the word *cent*. A *cent* is a piece of money, often called a penny. See the use of these homonyms in sentences:

Mother *sent* me to the store.
Mother gave me one *cent*.

EXERCISE 164

Copy the following sentences. Write *cent* or *sent* directly in each blank space.

1 I have a _____ in my pocket.
2 Little Red Riding Hood was _____ to her grandmother's house.
3 A _____ is made of copper.
4 You can't buy a pencil for one _____ .
5 The letter has been _____ by air mail.
6 The undercover agent was _____ on a secret mission.
7 Each day she put one _____ into her bank.
8 Who _____ you on this errand?
9 The message was _____ by radio.
10 Who _____ this post card?
11 I found a _____ on the floor.
12 I _____ a letter to my pen pal.

"EYE" and "I"

Barbara wrote in a book report, "This is the part of the story I liked best." She used the word *I* in place of her own name. The *I* is written with a capital letter. *Eye,* which is the part of our body through which we see, is a homonym for the word *I*. In these sentences, notice how these homonyms are spelled.

> *I* write with my left hand.
> The *eye* is a very delicate part of the body.

To help you remember the difference between *I* and *eye,* please learn this jingle:

Capital I and e-y-e,
To me they sound the same.
For part of the body use e-y-e
And capital I for your name.

EXERCISE 165

Copy the following sentences. Write *I* or *eye* correctly in each blank space.

1 A cinder blew into Clare's _____.
2 _____ went for a walk with my brother yesterday.
3 The doctor examined his _____ .
4 May _____ please go to the movies?
5 _____ am in the third grade.
6 The eyelashes help to protect the _____ .
7 The pirate has a patch over one _____ .
8 My sister and _____ are twins.
9 Put the thread through the _____ of the needle.
10 Mother said, "_____ am very tired."
11 Six muscles move the _____ .
12 _____ am learning to play the piano.
13 The word _____ is always written with a capital letter.
14 Her left _____ is stronger than her right one.

Contractions

An abbreviation is a short way of *writing* a word. A contraction is a short way of *writing* and *saying* two words. The words *he* and *will* may be shortened to *he'll*. The apostrophe takes the place of the letters *w* and *i*.

EXAMPLE: Tomorrow, *he'll* come to dinner.

WORDS	CONTRACTION	CHANGES
he will	he'll	Take *wi* out.
		Put the apostrophe (') in.

EXERCISE 166

Copy these sentences. Use contractions for the words printed in italics.

1 Ask Father if *he will* go swimming with us.
2 *He will* teach us to say some Spanish words.
3 Ask Uncle John if *he will* tell us a story.
4 *He will* bring the book to school tomorrow.
5 Next Friday *he will* be twelve years old.
6 *He will* go to camp with us.
7 *He will* come back soon.
8 *He will* go to college when he is older.
9 Tonight *he will* finish painting my bookcase.
10 Mother, *he will* arrive tomorrow.

"WON'T"

Another contraction that will help you in writing is the contraction *won't*. *Won't* is used for the words *will not*. Notice how the words *will not* are changed to *won't* in these sentences. Learn the correct spelling of the contraction *won't*.

Oil and water *will not* mix.
Oil and water *won't* mix.

WORDS	CONTRACTION	CHANGES
will not	won't	Take out the *ill*. Put in the *o* before *n* and the apostrophe (').

EXERCISE 167

Use the contraction for *will not* in each of these sentences:

1 The nurse *will not* be here today.
2 My birthday *will not* be here for a week.
3 The airplane *will not* take off today.
4 There *will not* be anything left.
5 My cat *will not* walk on a leash.
6 Evergreen trees *will not* grow in that soil.
7 His mother *will not* allow him to go.
8 Winter *will not* last forever.
9 School *will not* close until June.
10 These flowers *will not* bloom until spring.
11 The train *will not* arrive for another hour.
12 These scissors *will not* cut this heavy cardboard.

EXERCISE 168   [Chapter Challenge]

Read this paragraph, and then answer the questions that follow it.

¹Cherie and her family had lived in New York City for five years. ²Now, it was time for them to move. ³Cherie knew that she would miss all her young friends at Parkside School. ⁴How unhappy she felt saying good-bye to them on Friday! ⁵Would new friends be waiting for her in Virginia? ⁶As the moving van roared down the street, Cherie turned and a tear fell from her eye. ⁷"Good-bye!" she called. ⁸What day can be sadder than moving day!

1   The proper noun that names a special person in sentence three is _____ .

2   *Parkside School* is a proper noun; therefore, it begins with _____ letters.

3   The mark of punctuation that we use at the end of sentence five is a _____ .

4   Sentence one is a declarative sentence; therefore, it is followed by a _____ .

5   The marks that tell us what Cherie said in sentence seven are called _____ .

6   The word *Friday* in sentence four may sometimes be abbreviated. The abbreviation is _____ .

7   The proper noun that names a special place in sentence five is _____ .

8   Every sentence in the paragraph begins with a _____ .

9   Name a homonym for *eye* in sentence six.   _____

10 Give an antonym for *young* in sentence three.   _____

Index